It's My Time

PRAISE FOR *IT'S MY TIME*

Wow! This book is like no other as it takes you into the heart of how one man has been impacted and used by God's relentless pursuit of him!! I could not put it down! I've known the Phillips family since before Josh was born and his dad was one of my best "Jonathan" friends! So, I've had the pleasure of watching Josh grow up into the man he is today. . . . With multiple stories and illustrations from his own life, he has masterfully communicated the essence of growing into a man of God—challenge, victory, disappointment, defeat, tragedy, mistakes, renewal, redemption—but all with the laser-focused goal of wanting to know and please His Lord and Savior. God has molded Josh, who always had so much promise, into a powerful instrument for the Kingdom to guide others to The Promise of eternal life through Jesus. *It's My Time* takes you on a journey that will shape and mold your heart. If you actively engage you will come out the other side stronger, more faithful, and better equipped to face challenges.

Jerry Regier, PhD, founder and first president of the Family Research Council; former cabinet secretary of health and human services to two state governors (FL and OK), and senior policy appointee with three US presidents, current professor at Liberty University

This is a brave book. I'm reminded that even with those we know, we rarely see all that happens behind the curtain, in the parts of the journey that drive the transformation of the heart. Parts of this story reminded me of Rudy or the Kurt Warner story. Others reminded me of some of my favorite character journeys in the Bible, the ones where endurance and humility turn into impact. Josh's vulnerability and willingness to share some of life's hardest moments kept me turning the pages until the end.

Michael McClellan, author of *The Sand Sea*

It's My Time is a spiritual awakening to God's redeeming grace. Over a lifetime of determination to succeed in athletic endeavors, Josh's faith story grew into what it is today. It reached a maturity that echoes Jeremiah 19:13, which promises that we will find God if we seek him with all our heart. No matter where you find yourself in your faith journey, you'll find this personal story of transformation a refreshment to your soul.

Andrea Ager Montalvo, host of Embrace Podcast, fitness trainer, and two-time CrossFit Games Competitor

It's My Time really hit home for me. I fully gave my life to Jesus in college playing Quarterback at Florida State University in large part to my Coach Bobby Bowden. I, too, struggled with defining my identity through how I performed on the football field and the lens people saw me through in a high profile position. Christ gave me a new identity—one that is rock solid in Him. God took Josh on a similar journey. *It's My Time* is a must-read, and I believe with all of my heart if you walk through this with Josh that Jesus will change your life too!

Chris Rix, FSU QB 2000–2004, FCA Director, FOX Sports

Josh Phillips has written a powerful book that invites you to walk with him through the most difficult sometimes painful seasons of his life. I was captivated by the way he wraps his story around the reader and tells it as if he is walking with you as you read. So as you walk with Josh through his story, you will feel his pain as if it is your own during the times of greatest losses and disappointments. You will be affected mentally and emotionally with the same anguish of betrayal you have felt throughout your life. Josh's courage will become your motivation to persevere regardless of the outcome. Enjoy the journey . . . I did.

Dominic P. Herbst, MA, MS, founder & president Bethesda Family Services Foundation, author of *Restoring Relationships*

I'm old enough to remember ABC's *Wide World of Sports*, when Jim McKay would say, "It's the thrill of victory and the agony of defeat." When reading *It's My Time,* I couldn't help thinking with each endeavor of this young man's goals, accomplishments, and yes, defeats, that God was training him for Kingdom work. Josh is an aggressive athlete, but more than this is his heart and love for the lives of athletes and their eternal goals. This is a must-read for all of us who press on toward the goal, the prize, of the high calling of God in Christ Jesus.

Sally Meredith, co-founder of Christian Family Life, speaker, co-author of *Two Becoming One*, and author of *Overcoming Woundedness* and *Ruth, The Story is in the Names*

As someone who has been working in youth and college ministry for over ten years, I know how vital it is for students of all ages to find a place and space, to be honest and forthright about their faith, struggles, anxieties, hopes, and dreams. In *It's My Time,* Josh Phillips shares his captivating story with a great sense of transparency, inspiring his readers to do the same. Whether personally at home, in a series at youth group, or in a small group Bible study, this book presents a fantastic opportunity for students to wrestle with the tough questions of life, faith, and the goodness of God in all circumstances. At the end of each chapter, Josh provides the *"Red Zone Check,"* which consists of a few thought-provoking questions intended as personal journal prompts or small group discussion questions. *It's My Time* is a phenomenal resource for student ministers looking for engaging ways to have deep and meaningful conversations with those they are shepherding.

Zakk Uhler, pastor of Family Ministries at Canyon Creek Presbyterian Church in San Ramon, California.

Who doesn't love a good story? Not just a "mushy, everything works out story," but a story of resilience, redemption, and reward? *It's My Time* is a story that shares the journey of a boy growing into a man, and a man transforming into a leader, and a leader becoming a servant of Jesus Christ. It's a story that will make readers laugh, hope, fear, shed tears, witness setbacks, and learn how to bounce back. There's grit and grace. Defeat and victory. At the end of it, it's a love story between my friend, Josh Phillips, and his Lord and Savior, Jesus Christ.

Clint Hurdle, former MLB manager,
currently running errands for Jesus

Everyone has a story. Josh's story compels, inspires, and testifies to God's faithful plan for each of us. I've trusted Josh to be a role model for the most important people in my life—my daughter and sons, who are now in high school or collegiate athletes. Encourage your student athlete to read two books this year: The Bible and *It's My Time*.

Dr. Anthony Randall, FCA GA Wrestling board member,
chaplain, author of *Practice Makes Permanent,*
and Lieutenant Colonel, US Army, retired

Coach Phillips, as I know him, helped shape my life and encouraged my faith. In my time at Cal Berkeley, he poured into me and my teammates challenging us to grow and trust God, even through difficult circumstances. *It's My Time* takes what he did for me and makes it available for everyone. I pray it impacts you as much as he influenced me.

Giorgio Tavecchio, placekicker for the Barcelona Dragons,
European League of Football, formerly with several NFL teams,
including the Oakland Raiders and Atlanta Falcons

IT'S MY TIME

Learning How to Let God Write Your Story

JOSH PHILLIPS

NASHVILLE

NEW YORK • LONDON • MELBOURNE • VANCOUVER

It's My Time

Learning How to Let God Write Your Story

Published in New York, New York, by Morgan James Publishing. Morgan James is a trademark of Morgan James, LLC. www.MorganJamesPublishing.com

Proudly distributed by Publishers Group West®

ISBN 9781636981192 paperback
ISBN 9781636981208 ebook
Library of Congress Control Number: 2022952067

Cover & Interior Design by:
Christopher Kirk
www.GFSstudio.com

To my ferociously loving father, Jerry "The Jet" Phillips.

You showed me how to fight for what matters,
boldly chase my dreams, repent wholeheartedly,
and daily walk in humble submission to Jesus.
I've taken the baton; I'm running my race,
and I will strike at least one more blow for Christ.

CONTENTS

FOREWORD

My first connection to the Phillips family dates back to the earliest days of Joe Gibbs Racing.

I met Josh in 1992, when his mother Judy, who worked with us in our front office at JGR, was severely injured in a car accident not far from our shop. Her injuries left her in traction at a Charlotte hospital for over a month. Josh and his dad, Jerry, spent all that time in a local hotel, visiting her daily, while dealing with the stress of having their lives uprooted during Judy's tenuous recovery. Josh was only eleven years old at the time, and I can only imagine how scared he must have been.

My roommates and two of my best friends, J. D. Gibbs and Todd Meredith, had a close relationship with the Phillips family and especially Josh's older brothers, Jacob and Conard. They brought Josh with them over to our apartment a few times and we played video games and did whatever we could to take Josh's mind off what he and his family were going through.

I still remember just how positive and full of energy this young man was, despite all he was going through. I assumed that was a trait he inherited from his dad, Jerry. "Big Jer" worked for us at JGR and had a big personality to fit his six-foot-two-inch former NFL wide receiver frame and infectious smile. Josh was like Jerry's mini me, becoming a great athlete himself, both in football and as an elite CrossFit competitor. But Josh possessed a distinct vulnerability that I found refreshing. I always knew exactly where I stood with Josh and how he was feeling—no sugar coating. Josh also communicated his thoughts with a clarity that's rare among men. As Josh matured into a Christ-following man of character, God has only continued to sharpen and develop these traits.

Josh's story is a testimony of God's goodness, mercy, and faithfulness. Despite countless blessings, Josh's journey has also been marked by failures, heartbreak, tragic loss, and setbacks that God used to mold and shape his heart. I am the father of three boys, and by the grace of God, they have all come to know Jesus and given their lives to Him. However, I plan to give this book to each of them in hopes that it reminds them to see God's hand on their lives as they read how God guided Josh's steps.

One of my favorite parts of *It's My Time* is the Red Zone Checks at the end of each chapter. Josh doesn't just tell you his story and leave you, the reader, as a passive observer. These Red Zone check questions draw you into the story, challenging you to think critically about what God is doing in your own life.

It's My Time is truly a testimony of a life lived for Christ. It is a great tool to encourage young, driven athletes to trust God to overcome obstacles and use life's challenges as an opportunity for growth. But beyond just young athletes, it's for anyone that has a desire to grow in their personal relationship with Christ. Over the years, Josh has become one of our favorite guest speakers at JGR chapel as his story resonates with many of our folks.

In my role as president of Joe Gibbs Racing, I've been blessed to observe and learn many qualities from some of the most influential leaders in the business world, and I share those in my book, *Taking the Lead*, which also shares my testimony of God's redeeming work in my life. Josh models many of these principles himself in his life and in this book. My prayer for you is that *It's My Time* will help you draw closer to Jesus and drive you to take the lead in discipling others to know Him as well.

I am so proud of Josh for taking the initiative to write this book and for being so vulnerable in the process. I know his heart, and after reading this, you will too.

Dave Alpern, president, Joe Gibbs Racing, author *Taking the Lead*

AUTHOR'S NOTE

To protect the privacy of a few of the individuals in my life, some names in *It's My Time* have been changed. It is never my intention to place blame or point fingers. A memoir is a narrative, written from the perspective of the author, about an important part of their life. It does not share the whole story because, as we all know, there are multiple sides to any story. This is a memoir detailing *my* journey through trials and disappointments as God developed me into the man I am today, transforming my heart for His glory.

WHY I WROTE *IT'S MY TIME*

I know without a shadow of a doubt that God called me into ministry because I wasn't looking for it. Nearly everything I had done in my life leading up to my yes to God's call had been part of *my* great plan. I believed I was on the right track because I had asked God to jump on board and bless everything I did. But as He led me into ministry, God made it clear that it was *He* who had ordained my path, not me. It was His gifts and His providence that had paved the way, not my plans or dreams. And I'm so grateful for that truth. It takes some of life's pressures off our shoulders when we know God is in it with us, leading us on righteous paths.

Whether on righteous paths or not, there are moments that change our lives forever. Moments in time that we remember as if they happened yesterday or even a few hours or minutes ago. When we think about them, it's as if we get transported back in time, right to that significant time in our history, feeling it all over again in our minds, hearts, and bodies. The good moments. The bad moments. The hard moments. It doesn't matter.

My life has been a series of such moments, each one building upon the next, as God asked me to join Him, making a way for me to become the man I am meant to be. I say *am* meant to be and not *was* meant to be because the journey continues—and will until the day Jesus returns or I'm brought home to Heaven.

Life's pivotal moments offer us much by way of choices, growth, change, and more. That is by God's design as He transforms us from the inside out. *It's My Time* is my God-story, my journey from a simple faith to life-giving intimacy with our Heavenly Father. From immature belief to an indelible faith that continues to mold me and give me purpose.

As we are transformed by God, it's important that we recognize and know our stories, learn to love our stories, and finally, share our stories. My hope and prayer is that by writing my testimony authentically, not hiding the worst parts of my life—or me—but sharing the good, bad, and hard, I can show you that courage and honesty create connections; connections inspire relationships, and relationships are the lifeblood of a life with Christ.

One of the first ways to glorify God and walk His path for you is to know your story. What is it that sets you apart from those who don't identify with Christ? What experiences, circumstances, and choices made you, well, *you*? There will be—if it hasn't happened already—a turning point in your life when you declare, "There is nothing more important than God" or "I need God over anything and anyone else." That is a watershed moment, the story you must know and ultimately share. It's your defining piece of HIStory, your God-story. It's the narrative that will draw others to your Creator as you're reminded you must disown your plans in exchange for better plans—His plans.

Once we know our stories, learn to love our stories, and finally share our stories—which is what this book is all about—we can own our God-story in a way that casts His light into the darkness for others to see what He's done for us and what He can do for them.

There's one more thing to know about this book: In football, the space between the twenty-yard line and the end zone is the symbolic area known as the "Red Zone." The reason for this may be that red is a warning color for the defense. Once the offense reaches the Red Zone, they are in prime scoring position. At the end of each chapter in *It's My Time*, I've included a personal Red Zone check for readers. This is the time for you to apply the Scripture and story from the chapter to your own life. It's where you enter your Red Zone with the Lord, priming your heart and mind for deepening your faith as you journey through life to glory. I hope you'll take the time to do this. It could change your life for eternity and help you learn to see the story God is writing with your life.

Thank you for getting to know me and learning about the story God has written and continues to write. I hope it challenges you to become the best version of you and experience the abundant life God desired for you before you were even born.

Josh

Chapter 1

THE CEILING PANEL

Embracing our vulnerabilities is risky but not nearly as dangerous as giving up on love and belonging and joy—the experiences that make us the most vulnerable.
Brené Brown

I stood at the bottom of the dirty rubber-topped stairs that led up and into the bus, sniffing the diesel's fumes, and for a moment, relished the opportunity I found myself facing. Any feelings of victory and of being chosen, and the hope of finally *belonging,* would last only a few more minutes.

As the new kid at Lake Highland Prep High School, with my duffle bag in hand, I climbed the steps toward the bus driver, turned, and looked around. In the seats sat two dozen or so guys. All football players. All ages fourteen to eighteen, plus a couple of adult coaches sprinkled throughout. A sea of eyes fell on me. "Keep moving," I heard from behind me.

I chose a seat halfway down the aisle, quickly realizing everyone was already paired off, already grouped among their friends. Lake Highland was a K–12 private Christian school. Most of these guys had built their friendships years ago—back in middle or even elementary school. Some had been together for nearly a decade. The murmuring started back up once I sat, and I vowed to forge my own new friendships once we arrived at the summer camp, the kick-off event for football season. It was my first high-school season playing football.

Earlier that summer, I had been invited to transfer to Lake Highland courtesy of the head of the school, Dr. Robert Mayfield, a friend of my parents. The school was known for its football program, and I had lofty dreams. When my transfer became official in the head football coach's office, Coach Rose shook my hand, threw me a T-shirt, and said, "Welcome to Lake Highland football." My chest expanded with gratitude and hope. Hope for change and a chance to build upon my opportunities.

You see, back in middle school, I did not have a football-worthy physique. I was an awkward kid, not overly chubby but maybe way too soft. I wasn't growing like my peers, and I ate more than my fair share of sweets. My mom used to make me cinnamon rolls for breakfast almost daily. And I gotta say, if you eat cinnamon rolls every day, you're going to get a little soft. The time came in middle school when I wanted to date girls, but I was unsuccessful. I just didn't feel like I belonged anywhere.

In eighth grade, I hit my growth spurt, stretching six inches taller that year. Finally, I felt a little more "normal," though I was still on the small side for the sport I loved.

Ever since I could understand the game, and possibly even before that, my dream was to play professional football. This dream made a lot of sense to me because my dad had played pro football—with the Bears and the Saints—and more than anything, I wanted to follow in his footsteps. I idolized him while growing up. Transferring from a public school to this small, private school after my eighth-grade year was part of my intentional journey toward that giant goal. It was well known that many players from Lake Highland moved on to the elite college level.

Despite being filled with high hopes and ambition, the start of my first year of high school at Lake Highland was anything but wonderful. Back on the bus, I sat and listened to the conversations between the other players, feeling very much alone. We arrived at the camp and were herded into an immense dorm room filled with bunk beds. To no one's surprise, I ended up on a top bunk. After all, I was a ninth grader and the new kid—already two strikes against me. I spent the day trying to get to know the other guys, the pool of players from which I hoped close friendships would soon grow. Conversations quickly turned to football.

"I want to go to Florida State. I'd love to be a Seminole," I told the group. "I hope to play for Bobby Bowden. My dad played for him at West Virginia." I didn't stop there. "Then my dad went pro. He played for the Bears and the Saints. That's my goal. I'm going pro too." I didn't say these things to boast. In my honesty and naivety, I was trying to make connections, share my dreams, be me.

My new teammates didn't see it that way. On the third night of camp, a bunch of them held me down in my sleeping bag and punched me in the stomach, chest, and legs; they ganged up to beat me and then left me alone, lying in my sleeping bag, with tears spilling through my tightly closed eyes as they scurried back to their beds.

Unfortunately, the backlash for being authentic and sharing my dreams didn't just come from the other players. One of the head junior varsity coaches—Coach Trask for the sake of anonymity—didn't like what I was saying either. He had played football at Florida State, but from what I gathered, his career didn't go as he had hoped. He didn't start many games, and the one big break he had earned didn't go well.

The night following the beating, a kid in the top bunk a few beds away from me pushed the ceiling panel up and retrieved a can of beer. I had no interest in beer. I had never drank and didn't have any plans to do so. I was curious about where he'd gotten it and what else was up there, so I pushed up the ceiling panel to take a peek. At that moment, Coach Trask came in. And what I had envisioned as a week of skill building, newfound hope, and opportunities disappeared completely.

Coach Trask motioned for me to come down. As I approached him, he accused me of trying to "break out" of the dorm. "Come with me . . . and bring your cleats," he whispered through clenched teeth. I don't know how many kids saw what happened. Most were already asleep.

At 10:30 that night, Coach Trask led me to the practice field and lit into me. For what I estimate to have been about forty minutes, he made me run and do up-downs, a conditioning drill often used for punishment that usually ends after ten to fifteen reps or has rest periods between sets. I did set after set and wasn't given any rest to recover. The humid air sucked me dry as my sweat dripped onto the grass. I was all alone. Using only a flashlight, Coach Trask punished me with exercise for nothing—for lifting a ceiling panel. He continued to justify the late-night workout with, "You were trying to escape." My pleas and denials fell on ears that didn't want to hear.

Then he said something that made my heart jump and fear settle in. "If you don't come in the first three places in the morning run tomorrow, I'll call your parents to come get you and take you home." In ninety degree plus morning temperatures, the team had been running three miles to "warm up" to prepare for the three-a-day practices the coaches held during camp.

I crawled back into my top bunk sleeping bag that night still drenched in sweat and completely exhausted. I laid in bed, trying to process what had just happened, and as tired as I was, I couldn't fall asleep because of what loomed before me. I was terrified of failing—and possibly even more scared of letting my parents down. The shame of having to be picked up from camp and the long car ride home seemed like more than I could bear. The night hours dragged on as I tossed and turned.

The next morning, the sun came up way too soon, and just as I felt the light pouring into the room, I heard Coach Trask's booming voice. "Get up, men! It's time to run." I quickly threw on my LHP football shirt as I stumbled out the door. I felt depleted and dehydrated, but I had to figure out a way to finish in the top three. As the whistle blew and we took off, I settled into third place behind two seniors. Through the first mile, a couple of other players strode up next to me and tried to pass me. The fear drove me to push through the burning in my lungs and the fatigue in my legs. I just couldn't go home.

The course continued to weave through the woods, and the path wasn't clear for those of us in the lead. Typically, a couple of the coaches were out directing us, but they weren't there that morning. I could see the two seniors I was trying to stay within striking distance of veer left at a fork in the path. I followed, assuming they knew where they were going. I had to fight to keep them in sight. During the last mile, I didn't feel the pressure of my other teammates chasing me down, and I kept a steady pace just a few yards behind the leaders. As we neared the finish, I was feeling confident that I had done it, that I had held my third-place position.

I was surprised to see several of my other teammates standing around the finish line drinking water.

What the heck? Where did they come from? I thought.

Soon, it dawned on me. We had gotten off course! The next realization hit me flat in the face. *I failed.* Tears filled my eyes and snaked down my cheeks. *Does this mean Coach will send me home?* I wondered.

Coach Trask sauntered over to me. "I'm not going to send you home, but you need to get it together," he warned. I did my best to do just that as I pushed everything down into my gut where I could seal it up and ignore it. I didn't know that the effects of what happened at football camp—the mistreatment from my teammates and Coach Trask—would seep out later, creating problems because while I had sealed up all the pain, fear, and anger deep inside, I never gave it space to be healed.

Coach Trask continued to ride me all year. A few months later, in front of other team members, he said, "You'll never play college football, and if you do, you'll be the guy that holds the ball for the kicker on windy days." His ongoing assessment of me was this: You're small, white, and not that fast. He routinely asked me, "What makes you think you can do this?" and many of my teammates stared at me, persuaded to wonder the same thing.

I know the sting of feeling like an outsider and how deflating it is to be told that you're not good enough. I desperately wanted to belong, but instead, I was abused. Some of those teammates that—for whatever reason—didn't like me, who took exception to me, never accepted me. I wasn't invited to their parties. I was ostracized and didn't have many friends that first year of school. The older players on the team called me "Jerry" in reference to being one of the kids supported by Jerry Lewis's fundraising efforts (someone with special needs). So I know what it's like to be ridiculed, to be bullied even.

It seemed to me that I had just moved from one hard road in middle school to a different long and hard road in high school. I wasn't a popular kid. Not at all. And I thought maybe I never would be.

It's not easy being a teenager. I had tormentors at all levels, including adults who discouraged me from full-scale dreaming. Not only was I discouraged, I was ridiculed, though the worst of it came from Coach Trask.

"You're not big enough."

"You're not fast enough."

"You're out of your league."

But here's a hard truth: The world does that. The world can be a discouraging place, and people can be unkind, even ruthless. And this is true for everyone, including those who may appear to have it all together—the popular kids too. Why? There is an evil tormentor that lurks, trying to disrupt, steal, and destroy. He's especially greedy when it comes to Christ-followers.

> *The thief comes only to steal and kill and destroy. I came that they may have life and have it abundantly* (John 10:10).

Thankfully, there were some positive influencers in my life during this time. First, my parents. They poured God's truth into me, reminding me I was capable and loved. They built a solid Christian home for me and my six older siblings to grow up in. We were taught from a young age the truth of the gospel, Jesus Christ's love for us, and that He has a good and perfect plan for our lives. I watched my dad lead worship at church and my mom serve as the consummate team mom and youth group volunteer. So I was blessed with an amazingly loving, yet very imperfect, family. I also had a youth pastor who mentored me. Joe Sims encouraged me to dive into God's Word. Unfortunately, I can't say that I read my Bible every day. I wish I had. Because every time I would turn to God for comfort and encouragement, His Word held something special for me. God speaks in lots of ways, but His Holy Word is the primary tool He uses to communicate with us. My favorite verse during these years was Jeremiah 29:11:

> *"For I know the plans I have for you," declares the Lord, "plans for welfare and not for evil, to give you a future and a hope."*

I wrote it everywhere my eyes might land in my daily routine: on the bathroom mirror, in my locker, in my notebooks, and so on. And while the plans I dedicated my efforts, heart, and soul to were more my plans than God's, I found peace and comfort in Scripture. Though these were words that God wrote to a specific people at a specific time in history, I clung to them as if they were His promise to me. This verse and the encouragement from Joe and my parents sustained me. I knew that regardless of what others were saying or doing to me, God had a plan for me. And I kept believing, even when the odds were stacked against me.

RED ZONE CHECK

1. Have you made a conscious decision to surrender your will and your dreams to Christ? Surrender. Submit. Those are not fun words for any of us to read, let alone do. Submission is the spirit with which Jesus teaches us to pray in the Lord's Prayer, recorded in Matthew 6:10: "Your kingdom come, your will be done, on earth as it is in heaven." What is one thing you can surrender to God today and every day for the next forty days?

2. Do you have a dream in your heart—or did you have a dream? One you've been told you don't have what it takes to accomplish? What does God say about the purpose for which you were created? Read Ephesians 2:10. Do you believe this is a dream that God has placed in your heart?

Chapter 2

THE BETRAYAL

Bitterness is deadlier than betrayal.
Mike Murdock

Despite the summer football camp nightmare, I was pulled up to Lake Highland's varsity team as a freshman, in preparation for the next season. I was the smallest kid at five-foot-eight, 125 pounds, almost a dangerous size for this level of football.

My size was put on full display in the playoffs during my sophomore year when we were matched up against one of Florida's powerhouse schools: Belle Glade Glades Day High School. Their starting fullback was over 230 pounds, and at one point, he broke into the secondary with a full head of steam. I was playing safety, and there was nothing between him and the goal line but me. I lowered my shoulder and tried to lay a hit on him but ended up flat on my back. He ran right through me, but a fortuitous and bizarre occurrence prevented him from scoring. When the back of my head bounced off of the ground, his cleat caught my facemask. It's not the safest way to bring down a ball carrier, but at the time, I was grateful. And luckily, my face didn't have to pay the price.

I was determined to make some major changes to my body before my junior year and finagled my class schedule so I could take weights [class] first and last periods. I started lifting twice a day, eating like a madman, and doing everything I could to develop my athletic ability. I carried MET-Rx protein shakes in my mini cooler lunch box. And I signed up for any and every speed clinic, football camp, and agility camp I could find.

My favorite Scriptures from middle school and my first couple years of high school continued to provide solace for my dreams that seemed far-fetched to others but not to me, including Psalm 37:4:

Take delight in the LORD, and he will give you the desires of your heart.

As a teenager, I believed in what God said about me. However, perhaps like many young Christians, I applied His Word to the life I wanted, rather than putting my trust in the future that He had for me. I composed a narrative where my big football dreams originated from a God whom I delighted in, and therefore, He would turn my dreams into reality. It was my version of the prosperity gospel. I took Psalm 37:4 straight out of the Bible, with no context to define its truth.

My relentless hope also came from my parents, particularly my dad, who encouraged me by sharing that he was a late bloomer too. Genetics would follow. I would grow, but for now, I just had to work hard.

True to my dad's promise and through my workouts, by the start of my junior year, I had put on almost fifty pounds and now weighed in at 175 pounds. Our Lake Highland team went undefeated that year. It was the first regular season with no losses in the school's history, and I was proud to be a part of it.

I regularly played on defense, specifically the corner position, but I was also the second-string quarterback. That was my goal—to be *the* quarterback. To have the game on the line and the ball in my hands. Our starting quarterback, Brian Hoffman—a guy who stood just under six feet, three inches tall and had a cannon for an arm—was a year ahead of me, and was admittedly better. He had already secured a scholarship to the University of Connecticut.

During the course of that undefeated season, Brian was injured during a couple of games, and I filled in at the QB position in the third or fourth quarter, with the responsibility of finishing those games ahead and keeping our undefeated season alive. It was every back-up quarterback's dream, to carry that weight on his shoulders and come out on top. In those games, I handed the ball off a lot, but I threw a few passes here and there too. And I accomplished the goal—two more *W*s to maintain our undefeated season. I had not only proven myself to myself but to countless others too: teammates, coaches, and those who watched the games.

I relished in the belief that my senior year was going to be *my time*, my opportunity to lead the team. This was why I had transferred to Lake Highland. This was why I had endured that first summer camp. This was why I had worked out twice a day in weight training classes. I believed it was my turn to earn those scholarships and realize my long-awaited dreams. In preparation, I attended Florida State's—my dream school—speed camp, as well as training camps at William and Mary and Auburn to grow and improve my skills. I had a laser focus and believed God was fulfilling my dreams because of all of my hard work and my intent to live out those Scriptures I kept reading.

A month before my senior season started, Lake Highland's offensive coordinator, Chris Rock—not the comedic actor but a coach I had become very close with after earning his confidence regarding my talent—called me into his office.

"Josh, I have good news and bad news. Which do you want first?"

"Um, I don't know. What do you have to tell me?"

"Josh, I'm leaving. I got the head coaching job at St. Edward's." St. Edward's High School was one of our rivals. My insides experienced the sensations you get when news guts you. Warmth. Heaviness. A rapid heartbeat. "I care about you, Josh, and I'm sorry I can't coach you for your senior season."

I felt sad and hated to see him go. I hugged him and walked out the door. It was good news for Coach Rock but not necessarily good news for me. A tiny seed of anxiety lodged itself in my stomach. I didn't know who they'd hire or what that would mean for me, but I would soon find out.

Perhaps my anxiety was more of a premonition, a foreboding of what was to come. Lake Highland had hired their new coach.

Coach Trask, the tormentor from my freshman year, ended up being our new offensive coordinator. He had been the head JV coach, so I had not interacted with him much during my sophomore and junior years. When I heard his name, my stomach dropped and then nausea set in. Nonetheless, I was confident in my ability to leave the past behind us and move forward. Chin up, I resolved to be the best player I could be and earn those scholarships.

There was a quarterback two years behind me that had started for Coach Trask as a freshman, and this QB would be moving up to varsity. Coach Trask liked this quarterback, *his* quarterback. So we battled it out in camp—this sophomore and I, now a senior. Grateful I had become a bigger and stronger player, I took the majority of the first-team (starting) reps during the summer and in the early fall camp practices, all the way until the week of our first game.

A few minutes before that first game, I was warming up, tossing the ball, when Coach Trask approached me. "What are you doing? You're not starting tonight. Go take your seat on the bench."

And that's how he informed me that I wasn't going to be the starting quarterback for my senior year of high school.

I sat on the bench, my dreams crushed. I was demoralized, despondent. I thought, *If I can't start on my high school team, how am I going to win a scholarship, let alone play for any legacy football school?* In my mind's eye, I watched my dreams slip away. Tears threatened while I stood on the sidelines of that game, but I only allowed them to be released when I got home that night, when I crawled into bed and wept.

I went through at least three of the stages of grief that night. First, denial, that this was my reality. *How could it be? How could all of the work and effort I'd put in lead to this?* Second, anger at my circumstances and specifically at Coach Trask. *How could he do this to me—and this way? I had proven to be the better quarterback, at least in my mind. I had won the job!* The injustice of it tortured me. Third, bargaining. *How can I change this? Can I go talk to the head coach and ask for a fair shot?*

The next morning, a new resolve surfaced. I had been taught to never give up, so in my head, I started to work out alternative plans. *I can transfer.* There were other private high schools in the area. But the season had already started, and I knew there were rules about those kinds of things. I considered it anyway. *Perhaps, I will have to sit out a few games, but I can still practice and win a starting spot,* I reasoned.

My parents were unbelievably supportive. Just prior to the start of my senior year, my dad had taken a four-month unpaid leave of absence from his job at Joe Gibbs Racing to be at every one of my practices and games. His career had him routinely on the road, driving a truck for Joe Gibbs Racing's show car program. My mom ran the program, and my dad drove the show vehicles for Home Depot or Interstate Battery cars.

Funny enough, I had my first driving lesson on the streets in our neighborhood in an Interstate Battery #18 Bobby Labonte Chevy Lumina race car that had been used in the movie *Days of Thunder.* It had been repainted, of course, but when we fired that thing up in our neighborhood, the sound made walls shake and heads turn. I don't think I ever got it out of second gear. It's a wonder I didn't blow out the clutch as my dad shifted for me from the passenger seat!

So my dad took this sabbatical from his job to be there to walk me through my whole senior experience, neither of us knowing I'd be benched on day one by this new coach. I was my parents' last child, last son, and I was the only son who followed in our dad's football footsteps. My brother, Conard, had played and had a lot of talent, but it hadn't worked out for scholarships or college ball.

I think a small part of my dad wanted to relive the football journey himself. My parents were hurt because I was suffering and felt my agony as they witnessed what I was going through with Coach Trask. When you're a parent and your child hurts, you hurt.

The Saturday night after I got benched, my dad drove off into the night. I don't know where he went, but my mom and I sat alone at the house. Though I still wondered what had happened to him, I finally went to bed.

The next day, when I came down for breakfast, he was back. He said, "Son, I heard the voice of God." Now, I have never heard the audible voice of God. He has spoken to me through different ways: open and closed doors, others speaking His truth into me, reading Bible verses, hearing repetitive messages and knowing it's God, and other ways. My parents raised me to be very careful about saying, "I heard the voice of God," or "God told me . . ." because we don't want to give any impression that we *are* the voice of God or have some special connection to God that other believers aren't privy to.

So when my dad admitted this, my heart stuttered. "Son, this has never happened to me before. This has never happened in my life! I was out last night, weeping and wondering what God was doing, trying to find some direction. 'Don't let my son hurt,' I begged Him. 'Please God, bless his dream and give him a chance.'"

Then my dad shared with me that he believed he heard God respond. *If he's faithful, I will bless him.*

"Son, whatever you want to do—if you want to transfer or do something else—I'll support you, but I believe God gave me this message. So I had to share it."

I spent the next couple of days praying about it and thinking through everything. I believed my dad, that he had heard God. *Okay,* I thought, *I'll stay at Lake Highland Prep.* I quietly decided to wait and see what God would do with it all.

RED ZONE CHECK

1. Have you ever had the "rug ripped out" from you? Perhaps one of your dreams was shattered or a sudden realization changed your perspective or life. How did you feel, emotionally and physically? How did you work through the surprise and the other emotions you had? Did you turn to God during this process? (Proverbs 13:12)

2. If you've felt or heard God speak to you, how does He communicate with you? Is it through nature? Others? His Word? Feelings of peace? Circumstances? Timing? Or some other way? Have you ever heard the audible voice of God, either in your ears or in your spirit? How would you describe it? If not, how do you feel about people saying they've heard the voice of God? Are you envious? Suspicious? Concerned? Explain. (John 16:13)

Chapter 3

THE MUSTARD SEED

In darkness, God's truth shines most clear.
Corrie ten Boom

Game after game, my senior year ticked by, and I still wasn't starting. Football is a relatively short season—usually ten regular season games plus a few more if you're lucky enough to make the playoffs. Some sports, basketball, for instance, have more than twice as many opportunities to play in games and get your talent on film for recruiters to see. Each passing game heightened my anxiety, and my dream of playing at the elite college level—let alone professionally—quickly evaporated.

In the fourth game of the season, we found ourselves matched up with our district rival Bishop Moore in a game that was televised locally. Knowing that media would be present drastically heightened my urgency, as I believed this was my best chance to show college scouts what I could do. I pressed hard that night to make things happen . . . and ended up having my worst game of the season. I had no offensive production, and my most memorable defensive play was a pass interference call that gave the opposition a first down.

My team played well, however, and we won the game handily. When my parents approached me during the post-game celebration, I was distraught. I felt like I had blown my shot to show someone—anyone—what I could do. My dad put his hand on my shoulder, looked me in my tear-filled eyes, and said, "Son, go celebrate with your teammates. Your team just won a football game, and this is not about you!" I reluctantly pulled myself together, snapped out of my pity party, and went to congratulate some of my teammates on their performances.

After that game, I fought to get on the field in every imaginable way, taking offensive snaps at the fullback and even tight end positions. One of the primary ways I contributed was to "load block" on defensive ends during our option edge run plays. Load blocking is a form of cut blocking where one launches himself at the outside leg of the opposing end—in my case, someone who usually outweighed me by twenty to thirty pounds. It's not glamorous work, but it was physical and allowed me to take out my aggression, born from the frustration of being benched as a senior QB, a rage that continued to build inside me. I had been a physical football player since my growth spurt, but the desperation and anger that fueled me unlocked a new level of violence in my play. There is a difference between form-tackling someone and exploding through them, and I found the fury to flip the internal switch that made me a dangerous man.

This rage was further unleashed on defense, when our coordinator, Tim Borcky, moved me to linebacker from corner. I ran around like a wild man. I took my pent-up anger out on opposing teams and played with a fury I had never known before, unlocking something in me I don't know if I would have otherwise found.

I was a good, technical player before this, but fueled by my rage, I excelled in tackling. Our coaching staff made highlight tapes during the season, and in editing, they had inserted lightning bolts thundering across the screen to evince the explosive contact of many of my hits.

The load blocking and linebacker positions gave me an outlet for my hostility, but my desire to play quarterback and contribute offensively never waned. I went home after practices and prayed, seemingly non-stop, for my circumstances to change. But I wasn't physically idle either. I kept doing everything I could to change my circumstances while clinging to the promises of Scripture.

During this time, I faced bouts of insomnia. I couldn't turn my brain off, and I'd lay in bed, worrying about my future and how I could turn this around. Often, my prayers in the darkness would start out as laments. I cried out to God in frustration, wanting to understand why this was happening to me and asking God where He was in all of it. But as I lay in bed, calling out to Him about what wasn't going the way I wanted it, I remembered the clear faithfulness of God from the past and even my current blessings. I was healthy; I could be injured. I was still getting on the field—not in the role I wanted, but I could have been standing on the sideline for the entire game. I had a supportive home and people who loved and encouraged me. I wasn't all alone. There was so much for me to be thankful for. The laments turned into prayers of praise. I would end the prayers in a different heart position than when I began them, giving God the glory He deserved and receiving a small measure of peace in return. Sometimes, I would finally drift off to sleep in this state. But when I awoke, it all came crashing back: the fear, insecurity, and uncertainty. I bounced back and forth between these brief seconds of peace and the agonizing hours of anxiety. God was molding and shaping me in the waiting. He had something in store that I couldn't see.

In the fifth game of the year, halfway through my senior season, both of our scholarship-level junior running backs were injured in the fourth quarter. This raised the stakes for our next game against St. Edward's—the school where our old offensive coordinator, Chris Rock, had transferred to be the head coach. On top of that, in this next game, both teams would be playing for the district championship.

I know (now) through talking with the defensive coordinator, Tim Borcky—as he became a good friend of mine in adulthood—that the coaches had an emergency coaching meeting to decide what they were going to do at that running back position. Coach Borcky suggested, “Let’s put Josh at running back. He’s been the QB, so he knows the plays. He can jump in and do it.” Coach Trask, the offensive coordinator, was apparently against it. I was told they took a vote, and they all gave the thumbs up, except for him. Coach Trask had been out-voted. They put me at running back for the St. Edward game, and the head coach, Frank Prendergast, took over some of the play-calling duties.

They handed me the ball—a lot that night. I came close to reaching 100 rushing yards by halftime. I ended up with 125 yards and a touchdown. We lost 17–14, but it was an epic battle. Because of my performance that night and continued growth at the running back position, the coaches started me at running back for the rest of the year.

During the next five games—four in the regular season and one playoff game—I amassed almost 1,000 rushing yards, though a few were accumulated before I became the starting tailback. I ended up earning 120 tackles on defense and made third-team All-State as a utility athlete.

I don’t provide these statistics to boast or say *I told you so* to anyone. Yes, I racked up these numbers, but I didn’t do it alone. What I did was choose to trust God, even when I couldn’t see how this would work out for my good. Back when my dad spoke to me about my faith and shared the words he believed he had heard from God, I believed too. I believed that God was *for me*. That He had plans for me. That if I stayed the course, His course, He would show me what He could do with that small measure of trust.

He said to them, "Because of your little faith. For truly, I say to you, if you have faith like a grain of mustard seed, you will say to this mountain, 'Move from here to there,' and it will move, and nothing will be impossible for you" (Matthew 17:20).

At the end of the season, Coach Prendergast got up on stage at the team awards banquet and gave me the Most Valuable Player (MVP) award. Despite being benched before the first game, tormented and actively discouraged by my offensive coordinator, and ridiculed and ostracized by my teammates, God had been faithful. There were so many opportunities to give up and stop trusting God along the way, but I didn't. Before he presented me with the plaque, Coach Prendergast said, "Josh carried the team on his back the last five weeks of the season." That was a cool moment—certainly a validating one.

Please hear this: Again, this story isn't about how great I was. It's about how God allowed me to go through that hard season (four-plus years' worth of struggle, insecurity, and doubt) to grow me into a more spiritually mature person. To change me. To get hold of my heart. And He did.

In the movie *The Dark Knight*, Harvey Dent said, "The night is darkest just before the dawn. And I promise you, the dawn is coming." The original quote is attributed to Thomas Fuller, an English theologian and historian, who said, "The darkest hour is just before dawn."

It's not entirely biblical, what these guys uttered through these statements, but often, our dark seasons must be endured to make it to the light. And make no mistake, guys, the light does eventually pierce the darkness. *That* is biblical: The light is always victorious.

The light shines in the darkness, and the darkness has not overcome it (John 1:5).

The greatest blessings we experience in this life are often right on the other side of our trials. When we can't see our way out, when we're lost in the middle of the forest or stuck in a deep, dark pit and trust God to lead us through it, we'll see the light. The Light we have has a name: Jesus. And when we lean into Jesus and trust His goodness, we'll find ourselves in the most beautiful places we can imagine . . . but sometimes, it's only after we've been tried and tested.

Looking back now, I know that God really did me a favor. Better put, I had His favor. At the tail end of my senior year, I started getting recruited as an athlete by big-name schools: Princeton, Colgate, Yale, Auburn, and the University of Miami. I chose the university I did for faith-based reasons because, in the end, God's goodness and mercy had paved the way for me. And I wanted to honor Him in everything.

RED ZONE CHECK

1. Have you ever experienced or are you in the middle of a long, dark season now? How does it feel? Is there hopelessness? Despair? Anger (like me)? What are some of the thoughts that stem from those feelings? For example, in my anger, my thought was that I had to prove myself worthy of my dreams because no one else seemed to believe in me (aside from my parents). That thought propelled me to play with a ferocity I had never known before. It also forced me to lean more on God. What about you? What thoughts and choices or behaviors might be the by-products of your feelings as you endure(d) your hard story? Are they constructive or destructive behaviors? (Psalm 112:4)

2. Have you ever expressed prayers of lament to God? David had many prayers like this, which he expressed in the Psalms. (Look at Psalms 6, 10, and 38.) It's okay to express our frustrations and struggles to God, as long as we approach Him with the respect He warrants as Yahweh. He knows how we are feeling already, but He cares more than we can imagine. Is there anything in your life right now that you are wrestling with yet haven't talked to God about? Take it to Him; talk to Him about it. In the midst of that conversation, choose to remember when He has been faithful before. Choose to thank Him for what you have, even while facing the disappointment of what you don't have. See if God uses these conversations to change your heart position.

3. What is your opinion about the power of faith? A mustard seed is one of the tiniest seeds in the world, measuring 2.5 mm (1/10 of an inch) in diameter. Yet that seed grows into a tree. Why did

Jesus use this analogy? Is it an encouraging passage in Scripture for you? Why? What did He say could happen if your faith was even that small? What do you think God can do with a larger/stronger amount of faith? (Hebrews 11:1–40)

Chapter 4
THE TURNAROUND

God knows our situation; He will not judge us as if we had no difficulties to overcome. What matters is the sincerity and perseverance of our will to overcome them.
C.S. Lewis

I narrowed my post-high school choices down to a top three list that included Miami, Princeton, Yale. Colgate was in the mix for a while, too, but the thought of playing football for a Division I team—Miami—that had won multiple national championships was enticing.

The University of Miami couldn't offer me a full scholarship because of NCAA restrictions they had, but the head football coach, Butch Davis, brought me down during a recruiting weekend. Ahead of the trip, I wanted to be a Hurricane, especially since I had grown up in Florida. I wanted to test myself against that level of competition and play in the NFL, and I figured Miami was the best path to do that. Everything about it was what my flesh wanted, including the warm weather just a few hours from home.

And what an experience that weekend turned out to be! The trip was everything you would expect for a Division I recruiting pitch: cheerleader hostesses, locker room tours, jersey try-ons, and scoreboard introductions. On Saturday night, the Miami football players wanted to take me out to a strip club. I declined, but that decision was something that would soon influence me.

When I arrived for the recruitment weekend at Yale, the experience couldn't have been any different. I don't know if they planned this or not, but my host—Billy Artemenko, a back-up quarterback at Yale—said to me on Saturday, "Hey, I don't know if you want to go out or what you want to do tonight . . . if you want to go out, I can find someone to take you out. But I actually host a football Bible study in my room, and I'd love for you to come if you're interested."

A mixture of relief and curiosity flooded me. "Heck, yeah!" I responded.

That night, I met the other guys in the Bible study. In a little over an hour, these players were opening up about their spiritual struggles. There was a transparency and authenticity in these guys that I knew was the mark of the Holy Spirit in them. They supported and encouraged each other. It felt like a family and I already felt like part of it. I felt God nudging me, as if He was encouraging me, leading me toward His path for me. Internally, I battled that nudge. Miami still beckoned, and honestly, my parents would have loved for me to attend Miami too. They could watch my games, and Yale was the more expensive option.

It was not an easy decision, but ultimately, I chose Yale. I chose to honor what I believed was God's will for me. Before I even stepped foot on the training field or on campus to start school, and though I didn't know them well at all, I felt like I was surrounded by a brotherhood of like-minded Christians. God continued to build that community, by bringing AIA (Athletes in Action) staff member, John Hardie, and his family to serve on the Yale campus. John poured into student athletes weekly at AIA meetings and with one-on-one discipleship over coffee.

Despite never finding a church to plug into during my time at Yale, I was part of the Body and had fellowship and support.

That feeling sat in stark contrast to my high school experience. The dichotomy between kids beating me as I lay in my bunk bed, ridiculing and excluding me, to this experience in college, where, though I barely knew anyone, I didn't have to enter the community feeling like an outsider. I belonged because as the Body of Christ, we all do.

Once signed, I went into Yale's training camp as a freshman, recruited as an athlete with the coaching staff leaning toward playing me at safety. During testing, I ran the fastest forty-yard dash on the team: a 4.5. Because of that speed, they put me at the corner position. Again, what a difference compared to my earlier years!

The team was led by a new coach, Jack Siedlecki. Coach Siedlecki followed coaching legend Carm Cozza, who had retired after the previous season and would eventually enter the College Football Hall of Fame. The freshmen on the team were Coach Siedlecki's first recruiting class, and he liked to play young guys early, giving them experience, which freshmen on other teams rarely got much of. He was also known for winning.

I ended up playing in the first game (though not as a starter), and with that vote of confidence, all of my hard work over the years was again validated. There was another fast freshman on the Yale team by the name of Chris Larson. He and I would become friends and even roomed together during our sophomore year. That first game, about halfway through the second quarter against Brown University, we were getting badly beaten.

"Phillips, Larson, get in there." Chris went in at safety and I at corner. I got beat for two touchdowns by the eventual Ivy League player of the year, senior Sean Morey. But I still felt seen and valued by the coaching staff. Later in the season, I'd even snag a couple of interceptions as a freshman.

Yale ended the season with a 1–9 record. It was a learning curve—a valuable experience—for everyone, but especially for me. At the end of that season, before spring football started, the coaches brought me in and asked if I'd be willing to play running back. I wasn't super excited about that move initially, but I wanted to be a team player and help where needed. They had seen tape of what I'd done in the latter part of my senior year at Lake Highland and thought I could make a difference.

"All right, Coach, I'll do it if you need me too, but I don't want to stop playing defensive back." I knew I could start there, and starting was important to me.

"Okay, we'll see if you can do both as we head into spring training."

So I became the only player on the team that wore two different color jerseys in practices. When I was in for the defense, I practiced in white, and when I was in for the offense, I put on the blue penny—sometimes from one play to the next. It was weird (and comical). Some of the guys on defense found my color change a motivating factor for stopping me when I was over on offense. I became somewhat of a traitor for going to play on the other side of the ball. But it also offered me valuable experience, and most of us mustered up a few laughs over the competition.

In our spring game, I returned kickoffs and punts. I was also the leading rusher, and I played on defense, making plays there too. I got to do it all and couldn't be more thrilled. It was an exciting set-up leading into my sophomore year.

That summer, running back Rashad Bartholomew transferred to Yale from Air Force. He would eventually become Yale's all-time leading rusher. But going into our sophomore year, we split the reps in practice and sometimes alternated series in games. Even though we alternated, Bartholomew ended up getting the lion's share of the carries—for good reason. He was exceptional. I did get the privilege of closing some of our close games, with the ball in my hands as we were grinding the clock out. I knew how to hold on to the football, and my running back coach, Larry Ciotti, always said I ran with great "body lean"—meaning, when hit, I usually didn't go backward. I would continue to churn ahead for extra yards. That year, Yale finished 6–4. It was a huge improvement over the year before. We had become a much more competitive team. I made an impact on defense as a nickelback, helped improve our ground attack, scored a touchdown, and even threw one on a "Halfback Option" play against the University of Pennsylvania.

As we headed into my junior year, Bartholomew was still taking most of the carries at running back, and I was playing part-time on defense. But I wanted to start again. I wanted to fight to win back the first-string job at corner. So during the spring practice, that was my focus. It paid off. I knew I would be walking onto the field in our first home game against Brown as a college starter. I felt confident, not only in what I could do, but in our Yale Bulldog team. We were poised to do something special.

That first game against the Brown Bears was one of the wildest endings I've ever seen or been a part of! We were ahead in the fourth quarter, but Brown scored a touchdown and had to make the extra point to tie the game and push it to overtime.

I was positioned on the left-hand side of the extra point block team. When Brown went to kick it for the tie, our right edge rusher, Ben Blake, launched himself horizontally and made the block. My job, as the edge rusher on the non-block side, was to scoop up the ball, run, and score. But when the ball was blocked, it went toward the line of scrimmage. Brown's wingback, who was responsible for blocking me, turned and grabbed the ball before I could get to it. I went to tackle him, and I hit him—hard. I thought I had just won the game for us.

As we hit the ground, I heard the strangest sound emanating from the Yale crowd. It was a stunned silence followed by a collective groan. I peeled myself off of the ground, seeing bewildered looks on my teammates' faces. Confused, I saw the official raise his hands to signal a score. The guy I had tackled, as he was falling, had pitched the ball to a teammate—a lineman—who had caught it and run it in for a two-point conversion.

Brown had won.

After that loss, we reeled off one of the longest winning streaks in the country. It was an incredible experience. Going into the final game of the year, which was *always* against our bitter rival—Harvard—we had a chance to lock up at least a share of the Ivy League Title with a win against the Crimson in what we called "The Game" at the historic Yale Bowl. The Yale Bowl is a relic of a past era, of a time when Yale competed for and won National Championships, had multiple Heisman trophy winners, and even hosted the New York Jets for home games, with Joe Namath at quarterback. It was the first bowl-shaped stadium in the country and inspired the Rose Bowl and Michigan's famous "Big House." It can hold just over 70,000 fans, and on that blustery November day, over 52,000 poured into the Bowl's hallowed bleachers.

It was an exciting game. Our star wide receiver (WR), Eric Johnson—who later went to the NFL to play for the 49ers and married Jessica Simpson—had a record-setting day, along with our QB, Joe Walland. Eric caught twenty-one of Joe's passes in a game that went back and forth all day long.

On the last play, Harvard—down by a few points and still trying to win the game—heaved up a Hail Mary pass. My teammate, safety Ryan LoProto, intercepted it. I was right next to him, and when I realized we had won the championship, I fell to my knees and raised my hands to praise God. A bunch of crazed Yale fans poured out of the stadium onto the field, piling on top of us. I couldn't move. For a minute, fear ripped through me because I was being crushed alive. Thankfully, these students dispersed after a few moments. Once I made it to safety, I stood in awe of the scene, soaking up the victory. Listened to the roar of joy.

Noticed the number of hands thrust into the air in celebration. Smelled the sweat on the musty pads of the players and the grass we had trampled. I took it all in, and I couldn't believe we had done it.

We had gone from a 1–9 record to a 9–1 record in two years and had tied Brown for the Ivy League title. All of my hard work of the last decade flashed before me as I celebrated my first championship with my teammates.

RED ZONE CHECK

1. Have you ever experienced a time when you walked through something hard, only to celebrate afterward? Perhaps a graduation or something similar. Think about how hard work pays off and the feelings of accomplishment that follow. (Romans 5:5, Proverbs 23:18)

2. Creating an idol is believing that anything besides God can help you, or to hold something as more important to you than God. For a long time, football was my idol, specifically, my dreams of playing college and pro ball. Do you have something in your life that you value over God? The only way to overcome your love for idols is to be overcome with a greater love: Jesus's. How do you think you can be overcome with Jesus's love? (1 John 5:21, Colossians 3:5)

Chapter 5

THE IDOL

I would neither have you be idle in duties,
nor make an idol of duties.
William Secker

What drives you?

What do you wake up thinking about first thing in the morning? What stresses you out, making it hard to go to sleep at night? And what wakes you up in the middle of the night, drenching you in your own sweat or causing that knot in your stomach?

Odds are that you are basing at least some of how you feel about yourself—your identity—on these things. We live in a society that says we are defined by what we do, by what other people think of us, by how much we have, and by what we've achieved or gained.

We are all competitors. Whether you play a sport where your success is judged by wins and losses, faster times, medals, or trophies or whether you compete at the academic or corporate level, the world is built around certain indicators of success. It's likely you know those tangible ways through which your performance is measured; they may even be consuming you right now.

Being labeled a champion is a great feeling. I know. I was part of the Yale team that shared the Ivy League Championship with Brown in 1999. I can still remember when we intercepted that ball against Harvard to seal the victory. I remember it as if it was yesterday—how I fell to my knees and felt the cushioning impact of the grass, heard the swarm as our fans stormed the field, and cherished the excited cries of my teammates as we all celebrated.

But is that what life is about?

Achievement? Worldly success? Will victorious moments like these bring a *lasting* joy to our lives? And beyond? Or are they fleeting? Even self-limiting? These are worthy questions.

By the grace of God, there was more to my story than this.

During my senior season at Yale, our team was competitive, just not quite as explosive or successful in terms of wins and losses as the year before. We lost a couple of close games, finishing third in the Ivy League. While the team dropped a little in rankings from the previous year, I was a better player. I had my best year on defense, leading our team in interceptions with four total. My efforts placed me first in the Ivy League for defensive back interceptions.

Unfortunately, I didn't make the All-Ivy team because two of my Yale teammates in the secondary were selected. Todd Tomich started across from me at corner and had made All-Ivy the year before; he also became Yale's all-time leader in career interceptions. And our strong safety, Than Merrill, who would eventually get drafted by the Bears, was selected to the team. They weren't going to give All-Ivy to every Yale player. I understood that. These guys had good years too.

But I also thought I had deserved it, so not being selected as a senior was disheartening.

The biggest disappointment, though, was how I had to walk off the field for our last home game of the season. It was not the way I would have liked to end my college career in the Yale Bowl. We were playing our bitter adversary, the Princeton Tigers, in the oldest college football rivalry dating back to 1873. The Tiger's primary threat was Chisom Opara, one of the biggest, most athletic wide receivers in the Ivy League at the time. For most of the game, we had completely shut him down. I even snagged an interception in the second quarter when Opara was targeted. We were up by a score with less than two minutes to play when, suddenly, Princeton put together a drive that set them up for a Hail Mary.

I knew that with that little time left on the clock that the Tigers had to take a deep shot at the end zone and the odds were they would target Opara. Our defensive coordinator, Rick Flanders, called a "four deep quarters coverage" for our secondary. I lined up about seven yards off Opara and was determined not to let him get behind me. As he pushed off the line, I started into my backpedal, and before he could close my cushion, I opened up to stay on top. I could see through Chisom to the Princeton QB and noticed his front shoulder tilt up as he heaved the ball to the deep left-hand side of the field. It seemed like time moved in slow motion as the ball sailed toward us. I had a split-second decision to make: I could try to cut in front of him to intercept the ball, or I could stay on top of and behind him and attempt to punch at the ball and rip down through his arms to prevent him completing the catch. He was six-foot-three, with a big, vertical leap. Unfortunately, I chose the latter, which I thought was the safer play. Opara boxed me out and leaped high into the air to meet the ball. I punched up and made contact with the ball and then tried to rip his hands apart, but he held firm.

I got "Mossed" to seal a victory for Princeton. That was certainly not the way I wanted to exit the historic Yale Bowl for the final time. Before going into the locker room, I went back to the bench and sat down by myself. As my teammates left the field and the crowd exited the stadium, I stared out at the grass and reflected on all that had taken place in that hallowed stadium. I tried to rally my spirit with memories of great victories and big plays that I'd made. But I struggled to shake the feeling of letting my teammates down, especially my senior class, in what was their last game in the Bowl. It was disheartening, but I couldn't let that sting linger for long; we had one more game left against Harvard. I had to shake it off. Honestly, I was thankful to have one more chance to put on the Blue and White and suit up for the Bulldogs. I didn't want my career to end like that. Plus, I knew this last game of my senior year might just be the last football game I would ever play. I didn't want to focus on that possibility, though, because I knew it would heighten the stakes and make me too emotional.

I got another chance to show my coverage skills against the Ivy League's fourth leading receiver, Harvard's Carl Morris. I had a complete game. We held Morris in check, and we took the victory 34–24 at Harvard's horseshoe-shaped stadium. Once the final whistle blew and the game was over, the emotion poured out of me. My parents, my best friend from high school Brandon Yarckin, and lifelong family friends—the Regiers—came on the field to greet me and celebrate the win. I couldn't hold it together as the surreal moment unfolded. I moved from teammate to teammate, hugging them and thanking them for all they gave and trying to soak up every second of what might be my final time in pads on a football field.

A few weeks later, we had an end-of-year team banquet and Coach Flanders presented me with the Norman S. Hall memorial trophy. Each year, the Yale player that gives the most to Yale football is awarded the trophy. What does giving the most mean? I don't know exactly, but for me, I assumed it was because of all the different things I did during my four years at Yale. I played corner, running back, and on special teams; I was used as a gunner for punts, flying down the field on kickoffs, and getting hammer awards for blowing people up. Basically, I had done whatever they had asked me to do to contribute to the team's success. I felt honored by the award and the recognition for all that I had done, but what meant more was reminiscing about all we had accomplished as a team. My class, the class of 2001, Coach Siedlecki's first recruiting class at Yale, had gone from 1–9 to 9–1, won an Ivy Title, beaten Harvard three times, and made so many memories along the way. We called ourselves the "01 Rejects" because many of us had been passed over by high-profile programs and ended up at Yale together by accident, but nothing really happens by accident does it?

As soon as the banquet was over and the reality of college football being over set in, I immediately turned my attention to getting ready for the NFL draft. I signed with an agent—a Christian by the name of Kyle Rote Jr., whom I had been connected with through a family friend, Steve Hammond, who also worked as a sports agent but focused mainly on baseball, representing several top MLB players, including Chipper Jones.

In late December, a wonderful opportunity presented itself: playing in the Florida vs. US All-Star game, which is held in Orlando at the Citrus Bowl stadium each year. The purpose of the game is pure competition: the Florida players against the rest of the US. *Who is better?* This all-star game held a lot of meaning for me; I used to work out on the track and the fields nearby. The stadium was fifteen minutes from my parents' house and ten minutes from Lake Highland Prep, my former high school. I had been banging on every door, doing everything imaginable, for the opportunity to play in that game, one that featured players from Florida State, Georgia, Miami, Notre Dame, and more. After leaving several voicemails on the US team coach Buddy Ryan's cell phone—a number I got through my agent's and my dad's contacts—and after a US team player dropped out, I was afforded the opportunity to play safety for the US side, a position I didn't even play in college. And it was awesome!

It was such an incredible opportunity, one I relished for a long time. I knew NFL scouts had been there, watching everyone as the April draft day approached—then just four months away.

During my last semester at Yale, I started training for six hours every day. I made my entire life about getting ready for the NFL combine tests and trying to get drafted. I woke up, went to the indoor track to work on speed and agility, then moved to the weight room. My focus was on shaving off hundredths of seconds from my forty-yard and pro-agility times, adding reps to my 225-pound bench and inches to my vertical leap. Anything I could do to get the slightest edge on these tests and get the scouts' attention. After working out, I'd go back to my campus housing, a residential college dorm next to the gym, and eat as much as I could. I downed my protein shakes and trained as often as I could with my Yale teammates, Eric Johnson and Than Merrill, who were also doing draft prep and had signed with a different agent.

I was completely focused, to the point of neglecting all else. I wasn't even going to my classes. I had four remaining courses to complete for my undergraduate degree, and two of them just happened to fall at that time when I preferred to train. And since training was more important to me, I rarely attended those classes—particularly my history course. I missed the midterm, not even realizing it had been scheduled.

That's awful! There I was, a Yale student. I'd been given the opportunity to get a Yale education, but I was throwing it away. I was in danger of failing History and not graduating with the rest of my class. I approached the History professor and begged him not to fail me. The professor said, "Josh, here's the deal: We can weigh your final for ninety percent of your grade and the midterm for ten percent, but you have a zero on the midterm. So you'll have to make it all up on the final. That's what I can do for you. Good luck."

I attended that class for the rest of the semester. Some of my football teammates who were taking the class helped me try to catch up on the notes I had missed. The final was nearly all essay questions. And, thankfully, I did really well, earning a B-plus in the class.

That professor didn't have to give me that opportunity. He would have been justified in saying, *You're a Yale student; act like one*. Praise God, he gave me grace and another chance, which I did not flounder but worked hard to take advantage of. I graduated, but my priorities were still out of whack. I continued to obsess over trying to make it to the NFL.

The idol of football, and specifically of playing in the NFL, had a firm hold on my heart. Nothing else mattered, and God was demoted. I ate, slept, and breathed football.

I had a scheduled workout with some of the Northeast teams: the Giants, the Jets, and the Patriots. While the scouts watched, we went through pro agility drills on old-school Astroturf. During one drill, I tripped a little and put my hand out to brace myself, to keep myself from falling. When I did, my thumb was jammed into the ground, bending all the way back to my hand. Unknowingly, I had broken it. I knew something was seriously wrong when I couldn't make a fist, and the pain was excruciating. But the workout wasn't over. We had position drills up next, and I would have to catch balls thrown by the scouts, so I taped it up myself. There was nothing that was going to get in the way of me working out in front of those NFL scouts. With tears stinging my eyes from the pain, I did my best to try to move well and catch the balls heading my way.

When the workout was over and I took the tape off, my thumb had swelled to more than twice its size and was severely discolored.

Even though my thumb injury had prevented me from making many great catches, I had run well with a fast "forty" time of 4.45, and my bench was good. So I held onto the hope that at least one team had seen something they liked in me.

Several weeks later, the NFL draft finally arrived. I was giddy with anticipation, both good and bad. My heart vacillated between hope and dread. My lifelong dream was laid bare. I watched the draft from my dorm room for three painstaking days. I watched as Eric Johnson and Than Merrill were both drafted. And I waited, eyes focused on the screen while my lungs could barely expand, through the sixth and then the seventh round.

My name was never called. *I hadn't done enough.*

However, I didn't crack yet. I held onto a pebble of hope because I knew teams kept draft boards and would sign free agents immediately following the draft, those whose names weren't called TV but players they had their eyes on as potential recruits. But as the hours ticked by, my phone never rang.

The weight of the realization that my dream hadn't come to fruition hit me like a punch to the stomach. All those hours. All the door-knocking. All of the sacrifices . . . had led to nothing. I stayed in my room for the next couple of days, feeling depressed and surviving on cereal and protein bars.

It could have been over at that point. For most NFL prospects, it is. But I had that innate desire, an obsession. The idol of football burned in my heart. So I eventually peeled myself out of my dorm and got back to training as much as I could with my healing thumb. I went back to track work and managed to pull myself together and finish the academic semester strong. I'm proud and blessed to say that I graduated from Yale University in May 2001. After graduation, I returned to Orlando, moved back in with my parents, and stepped up my training intensity back in the Florida sun. Something about that sunshine always fueled me and made me feel just a bit faster. I peppered my agent to call people—then more people. I would not give up.

My thumb had finally healed, and I was running even better than before. My "forty" was now at a 4.35—though that time was logged while in track spikes on a Mondotrack. It's a fast, synthetic track for elite track and field stars, and even though it was hand-timed, it was a personal best and an elite pro-level time.

That number and my fitness level pumped me back up from the deflated shell I'd become immediately after the draft. Then, a call from my agent sent me over the moon. In early June, my agent was able to get me a workout with the Tampa Bay Buccaneers. The Bucs were only ninety minutes from where I had grown up. I was stoked with the idea that my dream was not gone yet. It had simply been delayed for a bit.

Two nights before the workout with the Bucs, I opted to get in one more speed workout with my buddy, Ivery Gaskins. Gaskins (IG) had gone to the University of Central Florida and played Canadian football. He liked to train for longer endurance sprints rather than just traditional football distances like the forty. That night, he wanted to run 150 meter repeats. I wasn't pumped about it, but every time IG was around, my competitive juices flowed. So I said, "What the heck," and hopped into the longer sprints with him. The first couple reps went great, and we were flying around the curve, shoulder to shoulder. But near the end of the straightaway, in our third sprint, I felt my hamstring pop.

I had strained my hamstring several times before in my life, but this time was the worst I'd ever experienced. The back of my leg turned deep hues of black and blue, a true hamstring tear. I was forced to cancel my workout with the Bucs, and my world collapsed once again.

The NFL season started in July, and I still wasn't even jogging yet. To say that I was depressed is an understatement. My lifelong dream, to which I had committed my entire being, had been demolished.

Many times, the New Testament warns of being seduced by the things of this world to where they become the most important things in our lives. This is idolatry. We see time and time again in the Bible that we—human beings with flaws, self-centeredness, and sin—tend to drift away from God.

> *Those who pay regard to vain idols forsake their hope of steadfast love* (Jonah 2:8–10).

I didn't know who I was without football. I couldn't even ask myself the question, "What am I going to do now?" because the answer gutted me. *Get a regular job?* The idea seemed ridiculous. Ludicrous. I was a football player through and through. It was in my blood. I wasn't supposed to be doing anything else. The world had rendered me useless, unable to do what, in my eyes, I was "made for."

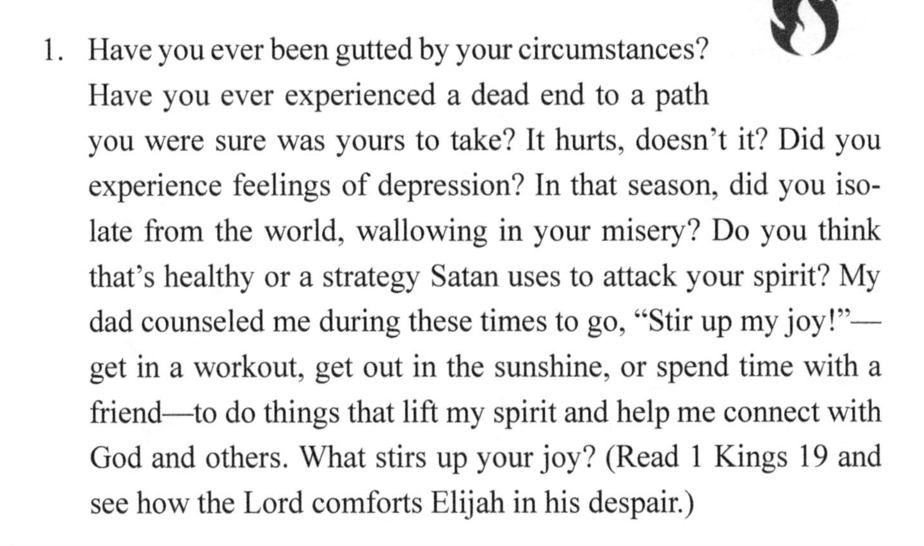

RED ZONE CHECK

1. Have you ever been gutted by your circumstances? Have you ever experienced a dead end to a path you were sure was yours to take? It hurts, doesn't it? Did you experience feelings of depression? In that season, did you isolate from the world, wallowing in your misery? Do you think that's healthy or a strategy Satan uses to attack your spirit? My dad counseled me during these times to go, "Stir up my joy!"—get in a workout, get out in the sunshine, or spend time with a friend—to do things that lift my spirit and help me connect with God and others. What stirs up your joy? (Read 1 Kings 19 and see how the Lord comforts Elijah in his despair.)

2. Have you ever experienced a time when God seemed silent or distant from you? Was it He that moved away from you or were you the one that pulled back? (Psalm 28:1)

3. On my side of things, I had demoted God by lifting football and the training and preparing I was doing for the NFL ahead of my devotion to Him. This caused me to lose my sense of self, of who God made me to be. What, specifically, do you think I was forgetting or missing as part of my identity during this time? In what do you place your identity? Where are you finding your value? (1 Samuel 16:7)

Chapter 6

THE REBELLION

The beginning of men's rebellion against God was, and is, the lack of a thankful heart.
Francis Schaeffer

As the NFL season kicked off, my depression deepened. I had no job. No real direction. No purpose. And I had no identity apart from football. I was living under my parents' roof, believing that life was pretty terrible. I had forgotten how much God loved me.

> *For the mountains may depart and the hills be removed, but my steadfast love shall not depart from you, and my covenant of peace shall not be removed," says the Lord, who has compassion on you* (Isaiah 54:10).

To help myself feel better, I started going out at night, trying to meet some emotional needs that had gone unmet when my football career had tanked. I didn't go into downtown Orlando to drink or do drugs. I wasn't engaged in any behavior like that. I had made a commitment to

God (and myself) in middle school that I wasn't going to be a partier. I wasn't going to be engaging in premarital sex because I truly wanted to wait until I was married to share that with my wife.

I had thought, *If I give God my promises not to drink, do drugs, or engage in premarital sex—if I control those parts of who I could be and avoid what everyone else seems to be doing—he'll give me the NFL.* I considered it my covenant with God. "If I give all of this up, then you'll pave the way to the pros, okay, God?"

God can't be negotiated with; He cannot be manipulated, and your life shouldn't be a bartering chip. We can't leverage God and His goodness for our selfish gain. The Israelites learned that when they lost tens of thousands of men to the Philistines in a battle where the Ark of the Covenant of God was also captured after the Israelites had tried to carry the Lord into battle via His visible throne, the Ark. They tried to manipulate God to secure their victory (1 Samuel 4). It didn't work then, and it won't work now.

The Lord doesn't serve us. His purpose is to capture our hearts, not our narrow-minded dreams. Instinctively and intellectually, I'd always known that. But back then, I was lost and spiritually blind to what I was doing. I was hoping for good fortune without understanding I needed a change of heart—a heart transplant, if you will.

When God didn't come through, I went out at night—a lot. Sometimes, I wouldn't make it home until the early morning hours. I wasn't drinking or getting into trouble, and I wasn't reneging on my promise about premarital sex, but I was hanging out with girls, flirting, and seeking some form of identity I could hold on to.

I was looking for validation, and the only way I knew how to do that was to look for girls to spend time with, hoping to find "Mrs. Right" along the way. By that term, *Mrs. Right*, I meant someone who shared my love for God and had a strong faith. I knew I didn't want to be "unequally yoked" in my relationships.

> ***Do not be unequally yoked with unbelievers. For what partnership has righteousness with lawlessness? Or what fellowship has light with darkness?*** **(2 Corinthians 6:14).**

In hindsight, my mentality was spiritually immature. First, I don't think I was going to find a faith-driven, God-fearing girl in the clubs. And I don't think any Christian woman would think I was living out my faith if I was hanging out in the clubs every night, either.

My parents never asked me to be home by a certain time. They knew I was a grown man, a college graduate, and at that point, I had lived independently for four years. They did, however, ask me to respect them by calling to tell them if I was going to be home after midnight. They didn't want to worry about me. I agreed. After all, I had just bought my first cell phone (no smartphones during this time period!).

Well, one night, I met a girl, and we seemed to hit it off. We spent the entire night walking around downtown and the lake, talking, and getting to know each other. By the time I realized it was well after midnight, my phone battery had died. I didn't care. We were having fun, making this amazing connection.

Around 6:30 a.m., I strode into my parents' house feeling pretty good about the evening, and I found my dad waiting for me. My mom wasn't anywhere in sight.

"Son, where have you been?"

"Out, Dad. Sorry I didn't call." My apology fell flat. I didn't really mean it.

"We tried to call you, but you didn't get back to us!"

"Yeah, sorry. My phone died." I shrugged, not thinking it was a big deal. The word *sorry* hung between us.

"Your mother is in downtown Orlando looking for you right now!"

"What? Why is Mom looking for me downtown?"

"We were worried—we didn't know if you were in a ditch on the side of the road or if something else had happened!" he explained. His voice had risen. My dad was mad. But I thought the idea of her looking for me in downtown Orlando was ridiculous, and I chuckled. I just couldn't imagine why she'd drive around expecting to find me in such a large place.

With my nonchalant laughter, my dad turned even more furious and moved toward me, and things turned from what I thought was a neutral or casual encounter to much worse—quickly. I had been working out and training for the NFL, so I didn't back away. I kind of bowed up, ready for the challenge. We almost went toe-to-toe. I didn't want to fight my dad, but I guess it was sort of an instinctive response.

"Son, you gotta go," he said, taking a step back but still looking me in the eyes. His tone had softened, but his eyes were still hard and filled with pain. With new resolve, he added, "You can't stay here anymore."

And just like that, my support system—the parents who had encouraged me during my middle school years, all the way through my college years—kicked me out of their house. And I didn't have anywhere to go.

Walking out of my house with my bags, which contained a few immediate-need items that I had grabbed from my bedroom, I felt a weird mix of emotions. My dad and I were still angry. On the one hand, I felt charged up and ready to fight because, from my perspective, I was a grown man, and I thought I was right. I didn't think I needed to check in with my parents anymore, and I harbored no regrets. In my mind, I had done nothing wrong. But I was disrespecting them, and I see now that I deserved this consequence.

Though my anger bubbled, I also felt an undercurrent of fear. I had no idea where I was going to go right away, so I drove around aimlessly for a while, thinking and wondering how I had gotten to that point.

The month before this all happened, I had befriended a guy by the name of Jason. We had met downtown at the clubs. He had played linebacker for a small college, and we both enjoyed working out. And we liked going out together. I didn't know who else to call as I drove around, so I reached out to Jason, knowing he had an apartment in a nice, relatively new area of Orlando. He agreed to let me stay in his loft.

The good news was that I had a place to crash, but I was miserable. Jason had no extra bed, so at first, I slept on the floor with a comforter. After a few days, my mom let me take their guest room mattress when my dad was out of the house one day. I put the mattress in Jason's loft, and then at least I had somewhere softer to sleep.

Frustrated by the direction my life had taken, I couldn't even watch football on TV. I didn't want to see it because it was a heart-wrenching reminder that my dream had been squashed. It quite literally made me sick.

This ushered in a new low point in my life. All of the things I had found identity in other than God were being stripped from me, and all the support systems that I had to lean on other than God had been kicked out from under me. I'm not implying that I, in any way, was a victim here; I was where I found myself as the result of my own actions and choices.

I *am* saying this was a divine moment in my life because it was God's great mercy that had taken me to this hard place.

> *No discipline seems pleasant at the time, but painful. Later on, however, it produces a harvest of righteousness and peace for those who have been trained by it* (Hebrews 12:11).

In God's great *mercy,* He allows us to be *disciplined.* Why? To shape us, mold us, refine us.

As I searched for meaning in something other than football and tried to find support from other places besides my family, I leaned into Jesus, to call out to Him in the darkness, to pick up my Bible and read, looking for His promises to me. I'd find them, but it would take time . . .

Amid this turmoil and the transition to Jason's house, I ran into a girl named Joy, who I had met four years before when both of our brothers had been in jail. My brother, Jacob, had a drug problem that he battled for years; he had been in and out of jail several times and spent the majority of my high school senior year on house arrest, living at my parents' home and forced to wear an ankle monitor. Visits to see him while he was in jail were almost always a terrible experience. The guards went out of their way to make visitors feel like criminals themselves.

A bright spot during one of these visits was meeting Joy, a young woman about my age. Joy was there visiting her brother, too, and we became acquainted as we commiserated over our mutual negative jail visits.

We crossed paths again at this point in my life and started to talk. In the course of the catch-up conversation, she asked where I was going to church. At the time, I wasn't. I had felt betrayed by God, and in response, had left Him and His Word on my bedroom dresser instead of at the center of my heart. Feelings are funny that way. They are not truth-tellers, only indicators of the *position* of our hearts in any given moment, and often, they are based solely on our circumstances. They aren't reflective of the *condition* of our hearts, the essence of who we are.

"There's a young adult group that meets at First Baptist Orlando. You should come check it out." Joy seemed to exude the meaning of her name.

So I did—I checked it out. After that first group meeting, I started hanging out with Joy and her friends. And I'm so glad I did. This group of people didn't care if I was in the NFL or not. They didn't care that I had played football at Yale. They thought it was "cool," but they didn't put any significant value on those sorts of things—the temporary, earthly things we all strive to achieve. The condition of their hearts was bent toward God, and it showed.

These new *friends* of mine—because that's what they soon became—wanted to go out for ice cream, go to the movies, and go bowling. They didn't meet at the clubs. They didn't traipse around downtown at all hours of the night. What they did do was love on me and encourage me, reminding me that my value is defined by Whom I was created in the image of and that the condition of my heart, the essence of *me,* is meant to glorify Him. They showed me the tangible love of Christ.

I learned through this group of young adults that people, young and old, avoid getting into trouble by surrounding themselves with Christ-minded people whose hearts are conditioned to love God in and through everything. They don't numb their pain or seek immediate pleasure by engaging in things that will never really fill the hole inside. This is the reason the Church (capital *C*) is so important. It's what a godly community is supposed to be. We need each other.

Through their encouragement and acceptance, over the next few weeks, I started to heal, both emotionally and spiritually. I opened my Bible again and read God's Word, seeking Him out. Because of this, I soon realized I had wronged my parents—I had been selfish and inconsiderate.

> *Honor your father and your mother, that your days may be long in the land that the Lord your God is giving you* (Exodus 20:12).

I knew I needed to apologize, so I swallowed my pride, and I went to see them. During the visit, my dad and I had a special moment where I looked into his eyes and told him how much I loved and respected him. I apologized because my actions hadn't shown that love and respect. I told him I had been selfish and inconsiderate, that he was right to have kicked me out.

"I'm sorry. I was wrong; will you please forgive me?" The words flowed easier than I thought they would.

He wrapped his arms around me and welcomed me back like the prodigal son I had become.

I had been gone for a couple of months. At this point, I had been struggling financially, trying to figure out if I was going to lay down my football dream and seek a different path or continue to pursue it—not knowing if that was even possible. As my hamstring healed alongside my emotional and spiritual life, I prayed through what to do. It was not an easy decision. My desire to play the game, put in the work to train, and fight for my NFL dream had not left me. I didn't feel led by God to set aside any of it during my renewed prayer life. So I decided to ramp back up and pursue my goal of playing in the NFL.

When my parents welcomed me back, I said, "Yes, I'd love to come back. And I want to try for one more shot at the NFL. I want to train again to see if it'll work out. What do you think?" They supported my decision, giving my dream new life.

RED ZONE CHECK

1. When your feelings get the best of you, how do you react? Have you ever turned your back on God or been in a position where you had to express godly sorry for the wrongs you've committed? What was the outcome? (2 Corinthians 7:10)

2. Have you experienced the difference between being a part of a group that does not point you to God and one that does? Are you surrounded by a group of people you can honestly say is a real godly community? If so, how have they helped you? If not, do you know where to find this type of community? (1 Corinthians 15:33, Proverbs 11:14)

Chapter 7
THE REVELATION

One of the reasons we minimize our own sin and rebellion is that we don't take God's Word seriously. Maybe a strong pinch is needed to get us to sit up and pay attention.
Kyle Idleman

My parents had raised me right.

When I moved back in with them, I wanted to earn some money to help pay for living there, reimbursing my parents for food and other things. I secured a job as a substitute teacher at Lake Highland Prep High School, my alma mater. Once I arrived, I asked my former defensive coordinator, Tim Borcky, who was now the head coach, if I could train with the team.

"I need to keep my skills sharp," I reasoned.

"Yeah, Josh. That would be great. You can help our kids and work out with us, but you can't wear pads—your helmet is okay. We can't have you making any contact with them, though. No hitting, no tackling." I agreed and started training with the team and teaching, all while living with my parents.

During this time, God did something incredible inside my heart. I had originally asked to be out on that high school football field for me: to help *my* chances of making my mark, to get *my* body into the best shape possible, to maintain *my* skills. Initially, I wasn't out there for the kids. But I often found myself coaching them along the way, giving the players instructions on technique that I had learned through my college years, talking to the wide receivers about how to run routes, and showing the players on defense how to cover their opponents, press at the line of scrimmage, box guys out, and strip the ball from their opponents' hands. I was out there for me, but in reality, God was having me give of myself to those kids. And I started to enjoy it. The giving of myself meant something, and I felt somewhat surprised when my heart was filled up by what I was doing with and for those high school players. I didn't know it then, but God was molding my heart for what He was going to do later in my life, which would be a full heart transplant.

One of the best parts of being out there, coaching and helping, was that it helped to take my mind off of me. And that's biblical progress for any of us.

> *Do nothing from selfish ambition or conceit, but in humility count others more significant than yourselves* (Philippians 2:3).

It wasn't long before Kyle, my agent, secured a workout for me with a Canadian team—the Toronto Argonauts. At the workout, I did great. My "forty" was a 4.45, and I ran a 3.8-second pro shuttle, but in the end, the team chose not to sign me. I knew they didn't bring many Americans up there to play, so I kept focusing, not taking it personally or letting it bring me down. Then, I got word from Kyle that the Houston Texans might be interested in me, a brand-new NFL expansion team. When I heard the news, my first thought was, *This is it. God, please make this be it.*

Charles "Charlie" Casserly, the general manager of the Texans, used to work with Joe Gibbs when Joe coached the Washington Redskins. Since both of my parents worked for Joe, I hoped he'd put in a good word. And he did. Joe called Charlie and asked him to simply take a look at a young man he knew who had played for Yale—me. It wasn't as if Joe said, "You have to sign him" or anything like that; he had just requested that Charlie have his scouting department evaluate me. Apparently, they liked what they saw, but Casserly said they'd only sign me under one condition: I'd be allocated to NFL Europe for one year first. NFL Europe was like the minor leagues for pro football. It doesn't exist anymore. Today, there are other leagues out there for players who don't enter directly into the NFL, leagues such as the USFL.

Casserly told my agent, "We want to see how Josh will do against stronger competition. We know how he did at Yale, but we want to see what he's made of when faced with even better athletes." Many of those players in NFL Europe were second- and third-string players from the NFL. I wholeheartedly agreed, excitement and hope flooding me again for the first time since just before the tragic Bucs workout that never happened.

There was a specific date in early February that teams had to sign players, or they could not allocate them to NFL Europe. In the couple of weeks leading up to that deadline, the Texans went completely silent. I called them (sparingly so as not to annoy them), but they weren't returning my agent's phone calls or mine. *Oh, my gosh.* I thought, *It's not going to happen again!* I wondered if my mental and emotional health could tolerate a repeat letdown. This roller coaster ride was not a thrilling one.

The days marched on in a tortured holding pattern, much like they did while I was sitting on the bench during my senior year in high school. I hadn't yet resigned myself to being done with my dream, but intellectually, I knew the likelihood was that if this plan to go to NFL Europe didn't work out with the Texans, it would all be over.

In the final days leading up to the deadline, I still had not heard from the team. I engaged in a lot of soul searching, desperately trying to trust God. I didn't want to fall back into old ways and carry my identity solely in my sport, so I battled, reminding myself: *You play football, but this isn't* who *you are.* This resolve was tested as the silence continued, and I became terrified.

> *Fear not, for I am with you; be not dismayed, for I am your God; I will strengthen you, I will help you, I will uphold you with my righteous right hand* (Isaiah 41:10).

Notice God's Word does not say, "Fear not, for I am with you, and I'll give you your heart's desires." No, that is not why we need *not* be scared. We can have steadfast hope and *fear not* because God will strengthen us and hold us up, *no matter what happens.* Often, it's in the waiting—and even in the letdowns—that we learn to rely on God for everything. After all, He's all we need.

Deadline-to-sign-day arrived. I woke up restless with the notion that if they didn't sign me in the next few hours, I was going to be devastated. Making the conscious choice not to give in to my fears, I went out to my parents' pool deck with my Bible and opened it, looking for Hope (Jesus). My mom stepped outside and, seeing my anxious heart, said, "Why don't you do something today that isn't about you, Josh? Get your mind off of all of this," referring to the waiting game.

Back in high school, I had been a student mentor for Best Buddies, a program for children with intellectual disabilities and other special needs. I had volunteered at The Magnolia School, which was located down the road from my high school, a school we had partnered with in high school to match kids for mentorship and relationship. Several of the kids I had befriended and mentored were still students at Magnolia, and I knew the teacher for that particular class was still working there. I had gone back during college breaks to visit periodically. So I called the teacher.

"Hey, it's Josh Phillips. I have some time today. Can I come by?"

"That would be great, Josh. Today is Special Olympics Day! So it would be wonderful if you could come and help the kids with their activities," she answered. We had a plan.

As I spent the next three to four hours of my day at the Special Olympics Event at Magnolia, I was struck by what I witnessed. I watched these kids as they competed in their track events, such as the long jump, sprints, throws, and other fun activities, and I noticed something profound. I saw the happiness they were experiencing by simply *being able to* compete. I watched their smiles stretch across their faces. I heard the giggles. I relished the comradery. And I felt their *joy* . . . and it was pure joy, with no strings attached.

God spoke to my heart in those several hours. Those kids didn't have the same abilities that God had gifted me with in regard to physical or athletic skill. But they were thankful. They were out there having a blast! And it was as if God had hit me over the head with a two-by-four of understanding.

I had begrudged God as if He had held out on me in some way over the past several months, maybe even years. I had continued to ask those accusatory questions, waving my finger at Him. *Why didn't I get drafted, God? Why am I not six-foot-three and weigh 220 pounds? Why didn't you give me a chance, Lord?*

I asked these *"why"* questions as if God had not blessed me in those very areas in which I complained. Shaking my fist at Him, I had forgotten that *He* is God, that He gives and He takes away. And that regardless of either, He is a faithful and good God who loves me beyond anything, including whatever I can do or achieve in football. I stood on that field that day with those kids, and with that conviction stabbing me in the heart, but the pain it produced was a *good pain.*

I have been so selfish! I thought with regret.

For those few hours, I forgot about the signing deadline, about whether it was going to happen. I focused on being in the moment with those kids. And it was glorious. Their joy became my joy.

When the cares of my heart are many, your consolations cheer my soul (Psalm 94:19).

Toward the end of the day, as I finally left, I looked at my watch, and it was just after 3:00 p.m. The school was in a cell phone dead zone, and unknowingly, I'd had no reception for the entire afternoon. When I drove off campus, my phone started buzzing with the notifications of twenty-seven missed calls, texts, and voicemails from my mom, my dad, my agent Kyle, and even Charley Casserly. I checked Charley Casserly's message first. As I listened to his voice, telling me he wanted me to be a Houston Texan, that a contract had been FedEx-ed to my house to sign and fax back by five o'clock, and that I would be allocated to the Amsterdam Admirals in NFL Europe, I pulled over to the side of the road.

And I wept. God had come through for me, at the very last hour, in a way that I knew it was from Him and Him alone. I had worked hard—yes—but He had opened doors and provided me with this golden opportunity.

Hope deferred makes the heart sick, but a desire fulfilled is a tree of life (Proverbs 13:12).

My time at Yale was an exciting season in my life that I'll cherish forever. However, if that was all my life was about, I'd be a *has-been* forever. By the grace of God, there was a lot more to my story than my high school and college experiences.

I knew at the time that I had been lucky to play both offense and defense in college, leading me on the path toward my next super-sized goal: playing in the NFL. Looking back, I know God had orchestrated the entire journey, particularly the positions I had played—both the ones I wanted and the ones I was forced to take that seemed, at the time, like detours or closed doors, including the door of playing quarterback.

In reality, I would have been an undersized QB. There are a handful of successful small quarterbacks—Drew Brees for one—in the league today. Most QBs are huge, strong guys that stand over six-foot-three and weigh in the 215–225-pound range—like Cam Newton and Justin Herbert. At that size, they can handle the ferocity and physicality of the game. As I write this, in the 2021 season, the tallest quarterback in the league is New York Giants' backup Mike Glennon, who is six-foot-seven-inches tall.

I soon understood that my twisting and frustrating path was actually an *answer* to prayer. God was, in fact, providing me with what I asked for—the possibility of playing in the NFL—by moving me away from the QB position, but I also understand now that God was trying to develop my faith too. And that second divine purpose of His is always the more important one. He allowed me to go through those tough circumstances to deepen my dependence on Him. We all need to depend on God, no matter how well things are going in life.

Think of King David. He had been anointed king decades before that position became his reality. First, though, he was forced to travel a rocky road that likely caused him to believe he was moving in the wrong direction, particularly when he was forced to run for his life and hide in caves. What that challenging path ended up doing was intensifying his relationship with and devotion to God.

Like David, this path was changing and reorienting my heart to want His way more than mine. To desire a relationship with Him above achievement or things. That was the point of my high school and college experience. I consistently felt I was being short-changed, that God wasn't giving me the things I had worked so hard for. I thought my dreams were being denied. But like David, I continued to believe that God was good, that He was able, and one day, if I kept honoring Him with my life, and doing everything I could to maximize my ability, it would end victoriously—in the NFL. I continued to pray and read His Word. On His end, God was turning me toward Him for His own plans, preparing me for the responsibilities He would entrust me with, even though I wouldn't realize that for years to come . . .

No matter what earthly position you find yourself in, if you're turned toward God, you're in the right place, and He can do great things through and for you.

Admittedly, I leaned on God a lot, but often, I didn't get everything right. Of course, I didn't see all that God was doing and certainly didn't anticipate what would happen later because of my self-focused goals. The truth was football had become an idol for me, and it remained one for quite some time, even after my Yale career.

> *You shall not make for yourself a carved image, or any likeness of anything that is in heaven above, or that is in the earth beneath, or that is in the water under the earth. You shall not bow down to them or serve them, for I the Lord your God am a jealous God, visiting the iniquity of the fathers on the children to the third and the fourth generation of those who hate me . . .* (Exodus 20:4–5).

Because of my wayward priorities, God continued to pave the way for even more growth. I needed it. God would continue to mold me to become the man He had designed me to be.

I thanked God for His faithfulness, and *then* I rushed home. It was one of the most overwhelming days of my life—not only because God's goodness paved my way to the NFL, but even more so, because His goodness opened my eyes to all of the blessings He had *already* given me along the way.

RED ZONE CHECK

1. Have you had an "aha" moment like the one I described during Special Olympics Day at The Magnolia School? What was the lesson, and is it still pertinent to your life today? (Isaiah 50:4)

2. In the First Book of Samuel, Chapter Seven, Israel was victorious over the Philistines, and it was decisive; though, it shouldn't have been. To commemorate the victory, "Samuel took a stone and set it up between Mizpah and Shen. He named it Ebenezer, saying, 'Thus far, the LORD has helped us" (verse 12). Ebenezer means "stone of help." From then on, every time an Israelite saw the stone erected by Samuel, he would have a tangible reminder of the Lord's power and protection. The "stone of help" marked the spot where the enemy had been routed, and God's promise to bless His repentant people had been honored. How has God been faithful to you? Are you slow to give thanks? I encourage you to either list out all of the ways God's goodness has affected your life or set up an Ebenezer to remind you of His goodness.

Chapter 8

THE NICKNAME

He (God) usually prefers to work through people rather than perform miracles, so that we will depend on each other for fellowship.
Rick Warren

It's not easy to keep your dreams alive, especially when obstacles block so many parts of the journey. I entered training camp on the most positive note possible, on the heels of a spiritual "aha" moment.

All of the teams in NFL Europe—the Scottish Claymores, the Barcelona Dragons, the Berlin Thunder, the Rhein Fire, and Frankfurt Galaxy—held their training camps in Tampa, Florida. My road to the NFL, yet again, led me back to Tampa, where the Amsterdam Admirals practiced at the Bucs training facility. Less than a year after my terrible hamstring tear that cost me a workout with the Buccaneers, I was using their locker rooms, practicing on their field, and playing NFL Europe scrimmages in Raymond James Stadium. I was in awe of the journey He had taken me on and of His goodness!

The Admirals roster opened training camp with thirteen defensive backs (DBs). And these were big-time players from big-time schools: USC, Notre Dame, Florida, Georgia, and others. As a white DB, a cornerback, from Yale, I was an anomaly. The last time a white corner started a game in the NFL had been Jason Sehorn, which had been back in the early 2000s.

After the first couple of weeks, the coaches moved me to safety. They also told us that of the thirteen DBs, they'd only keep six for NFL Europe; the rest would be cut. We all heard the message: The odds were not great. As the weeks progressed, I remembered Charley Casserly's motivating words to me when he said, "We want to see you against a higher level of competition." The competition was definitely fierce.

My roommate assignment, a DB named Blaine McElmurry, became an incredible blessing to me. He had been to NFL Europe before and had garnered wisdom from his previous NFL experience with the Green Bay Packers and Jacksonville Jaguars. Blaine was a cerebral guy and a Christ-follower. We could talk about our faith openly, and he helped me with the *X*s and *O*s of the transition to safety. He didn't have to help me. We were in competition with each other for a few coveted spots. He could have decided, "I don't want this guy to make the team in front of me," and avoided me, but he didn't. Instead, he helped me figure out the playbook and mentored me about the nuances of the safety position. After all, I hadn't played safety since the all-star game with Buddy Ryan as coach.

We prayed together often, and Blaine pointed me to God, reminding me to focus on my identity in Him as each round of cuts came up. Yes, *each round.* There were several scheduled cuts along the way to whittle us down from thirteen to six DBs. For each round, the coaches told us to wait in our rooms between a certain span of time (e.g., from 4:00–6:00 p.m.). If the coaches were cutting us, we'd get a call. Every one of these one- or two-hour windows felt awful. We DBs just sat in our rooms, pacing, trying to find a distraction while waiting and hoping our phones would not ring.

To avoid those calls, I played my guts out day in and day out, doing everything I could to be deemed valuable. I made a lot of plays on special teams: blocking field goals, busting the wedge on kickoffs, blocking punts. I played like a guy with his hair on fire, my level of effort utterly insane—so much so, one of my teammates, Mike Sutton, a big defensive lineman, started calling me "Crazy White."

"You're just a crazy white boy, running around and slamming into stuff. We're not even supposed to be tackling right now," he told me once.

On the inside, I thought, *Man, I have to give everything I have for this chance. So that's what I'm doing!*

With every cut, my heart raced and my insides twisted uncomfortably. The group had dwindled down, and I had made it to the last round of cuts. I was still there. Truthfully, I didn't think I was going to make it past this last round. Some might call it fear (and it was). Others may even recognize it as a by-product of the rejection I experienced during the NFL draft (and it was that too).

In an effort to ease my obvious emotional burden, as we sat in our room during the designated "window of terror," Blaine turned to me and said, "Josh, you're going to be okay." He was telling me, *I think you're going to make it.* I didn't have the same level of confidence or peace he did, but I leaned into God and tried not to put my identity into the outcome. I reminded myself of my friends at Best Buddies. I reminded myself that no matter what, God loves me and has a plan for me. Then, I tried not to stare at the phone for the next sixty minutes.

That phone never rang. Crazy White had made it through.

As one of the six DBs on the Amsterdam Admirals, I experienced Europe as a pro football player. The team stayed in a five-star hotel for four months. Monday through Friday, our practices were scheduled from morning to early afternoon, and then we had the rest of the day free. Blaine and I joined the football Bible study that took place in the evenings, a gathering of five to ten guys who regularly showed up to dive into God's Word. It was a time to lift each other up in the Spirit, and it buoyed my spiritual and emotional health.

Our coach, Bart Andrus, gave us a couple of four-day weekends while we were on the road to sightsee and tour around other parts of Europe. It was honestly one of the best experiences of my life. As my faith grew and my football goals progressed toward my ultimate dream, all seemed "right" in my world.

We all know the faith journey encompasses highs and lows, peaks and valleys. This was, undoubtedly, one of the peaks.

In the first couple of games in NFL Europe, I played the safety position, but I didn't start. I made plays on special teams, in nickel situations, or was subbed into the game. One interesting part of it all was that I became the first player to ever play a professional snap for the Houston Texans franchise because NFL Europe's season runs ahead of the NFL season. I got to be on the opening kick-off of the first game, so I hold a unique distinction. It's a cool memory that I'll always treasure and I guess also a random trivia fact I can use in the future.

We went 2–0 to start the season and had high hopes of winning an NFL Europe league title. Our roster boasted veteran leadership, with players like Blaine and our QB, Kevin Daft. Kevin, who was also part of our Bible study group, had logged some NFL time with the Tennessee Titans and played in NFL Europe before this. He ran our offense like a true pro and always seemed poised under pressure.

Unfortunately, our championship aspirations came crashing down when we lost game three to the Barcelona Dragons and Daft was crushed on a sack, injuring his shoulder and neck. It was a colossal blow to all of us and took some of the excitement out of our sails. We had spent the night before the game at the team hotel, which was at a picturesque location facing the beaches of Barcelona. There had been rumors that Coach Andrus would let us stay an extra night to explore the city after a win. But after that discouraging defeat, Coach told us to load up the team bus—that we were heading back. It was a long, somber, quiet ride back to Amsterdam.

During that game in Barcelona, Kevin wasn't the only one injured. Our starting safety, Ray Perryman, and Blaine were both nicked up as well. Our defensive backs coach, Jeff Reinebold, informed me I would get my first professional start the next week as the Berlin Thunder came to Amsterdam.

That week during practice, excitement coursed through me, every nerve on fire. It was the chance I had been waiting to experience for a decade—longer, even. We had a three-day weekend going into our matchup, and the coach let us do whatever we wanted—travel if we chose to do so. Some of the guys in my Bible study took a speed train down to Paris. I wanted to go, but I knew this was my first pro start in NFL Europe, and I wanted to make sure I was ready. So I stayed behind and watch extra film that weekend and ensure I was mentally locked in for this opportunity.

I had a decent game at safety, but we lost, the second in a streak of six straight losses that torpedoed our season. It wasn't the season any of us hoped for, and as the losing streak mounted, we searched for reasons to stay motivated. We found it in week nine when the Barcelona Dragons came to play us at home. Remember, the Dragons had handed us our first loss and taken out our QB and several other key players in a demoralizing loss back six weeks earlier. So this was a revenge game for us, but I had a personal motivation as well. Than Merrill, my former Yale teammate, who I had lined up next to for three years at Yale, was playing for the Dragons. In our first matchup, I hadn't had much playing time, but this time, I was a starter. We both played defense, so this wasn't really a direct matchup, but we did go head-to-head on a couple of special teams' plays. I would like to think I got the better of that matchup. I'm sure Than would tell a different story. But the Admirals got the *W*, and I intercepted former Ohio State starting QB Joe Germaine. Joe not only won a Rose Bowl at Ohio State, but he earned a Super Bowl ring with the Rams in 2000. Picking off Joe was a memorable moment. I kept the ball as a keepsake . . . and I still have it.

We had some epic battles against great teams, but for me, the highlight—besides just getting to play at that level and see Europe—was the bond I formed with the guys in the Bible study, a solid group of believers.

After the season, I flew to Houston for a brief layover to get my physical done for the Texans. I was still nursing and rehabbing an injured rotator cuff I sustained in Europe, but I was cleared. After flying back to Florida, I had a month and a half to train, prepare, and get my shoulder injury completely healed before the next season would start again. And again, I worked my butt off.

In 2002, I arrived at the Houston Texans training camp. It was the first season of the David Carr era; he had been their first-round draft pick. As soon as the team liaison picked me up at the airport, he took me to the hotel right next to the Texans' brand-new stadium and practice facilities. My heart skipped a beat or two as I looked at what I hoped would be my new "work home."

I roomed with a punter who had also been in NFL Europe. After checking-in and dropping my bags, I went to my first meal of training camp. Sitting at the table, I looked at the faces of a couple of guys that were already NFL legends to me: Aaron Glenn and Marcus Coleman, to name just two. These guys were corners that had been with the Jets. Aaron was a smaller corner, smart and talented. Marcus was big, lanky, and crazy-athletic, someone normally tasked with covering the bigger wide receivers. Aaron, who is now the defensive coordinator for the Detroit Lions, was really kind to me. Marcus was too, but Aaron took the time to get to know me.

What a surreal experience God had led me to in this season of my life. He had surrounded me with an incredible Christian football family and a talented group of athletes. Many of them hoped to be used in their current position to make an impact for His Kingdom. I realized I was one of them.

RED ZONE CHECK

1. Have you ever experienced a surreal moment or season in your life when you knew God's blessings were over you? What was that moment like? How did you know it was God's blessing and provision that you were experiencing? (Psalms 84:11, Psalms 90:17)

2. Have you ever been a part of a Christian small group where you felt you belonged? That you were making an impact on those around you or, at least, growing in your faith to, someday, make a big impact? How did that feel? (1 Corinthians 12:12)

Chapter 9

THE TEXANS

God has given me so much in my young life. I am truly blessed. But now I find myself at a critical junction . . .
My Journal Entry, July 13, 2002

That first day at the Texans training camp brought a conditioning test like I'd never experienced. Looking back, I see how it could have been the hardest conditioning tests ever created, at least from an elite athleticism standpoint.

We had to run twenty-four forty-yard dashes, one every thirty seconds, and each position group had a time to make. The DBs had to make them all in under 4.6 seconds. Now, that's a fast time for most college skilled players. To repeat that over and over, with only a short rest, was no easy task.

Running a 4.6 requires 90 to 95 percent of your maximum effort. To maintain that energy and output for two sets of twelve, in 105-degree heat in Houston, Texas of all places, was an enormous challenge. But it was one I believed I was ready for. After all, I was used to the heat, having grown up in Florida. The conditioning test revealed who was both fast *and* fit. In the end, I wasn't the fastest DB by any stretch, but my effort won me a few "forties" along the way. I prayed the coaches noticed.

Once we started practicing, I discerned rather quickly that this pro level of talent is a step up from even NFL Europe. I was learning a lesson: At every level I'd traversed, from high school to the NFL, the talent proved exponentially greater. Each time, I faced greater competition where everyone was *bigger*, *stronger*, and *faster*. At this level, I learned what 100 percent effort truly meant. I thought I knew what all-out effort was in high school. I didn't. I thought I realized what 100 percent effort meant in college. I hadn't. At the All-Star game? Nope. In NFL Europe? Wrong again.

I realized to compete at this level, I would have to go all out, every time. Unfortunately, I didn't get that many reps during training camp. In their first year as an expansion team, the Texans could carry more players in their roster than the norm. So there were more players in the mix. In the two-a-day practices, during what are called "team sessions," I was listed as a four, meaning I would only get four to six reps total during the defensive team periods. The starters, or the ones, had most of the reps, especially since we were a new team, and the coaches wanted to make sure the starters were ready to play. The twos had the next largest number of reps, and so on. As a fourth-string player, which most teams didn't even have at camp, I split reps with the threes.

One of the personal highlights for me came during our one-on-one periods with the wide receivers. On two of these plays, I intercepted the ball from the number-one overall draft pick, David Carr. The first was a "curl route" that I jumped with great anticipation. The other was a "deep out run" by Jermaine Lewis, who was a former pro bowler who had just come off of a Super Bowl Win with the Baltimore Ravens in 2001, where he returned a second-half kickoff for a touchdown. As Lewis broke out, I angled toward his up-field shoulder. The ball was slightly under thrown, and I was able to cut underneath Lewis and snatch the ball out of the air. My Texans defensive teammates were jumping up and down on the sideline and hollering out at Carr and Lewis. I ran down the sideline with a big smile on my face. I'm sure it wasn't a big deal to them, and they likely have no recollection of this, but for me, these are still treasured moments from my NFL journey. These show flashes of proof that I could compete at that level.

Since I wasn't getting enough reps (I assumed I'd need to show them I was worth keeping), when they put me on special teams, I did what I did in NFL Europe. I became Crazy White, giving it everything I had *every time*. My goal was to be noticed by the special teams coordinator, Joe Marciano, a reputable coach who had been in the league for several years. I wanted to impress him.

Well, he noticed me alright. He put me in for a play on kickoff as the "wedge buster." My task was to bust through three offensive linemen that would link up and roll, like a moving wall, to protect the returner. I knew where my gap would be; I was supposed to split the wedge between the middle guy and the guy on the right. During a scrimmage against the Dallas Cowboys, the kickoff flew through the air, and I took off. When I reached the wedge (the wall of guys), I leaped and dove over them, flying between the shoulders of these offensive linemen, and hit the returner to make the play. Some of my teammates sprinted over, congratulating me. I thought I'd made an incredible play. All of my senses burned, fueled by the adrenaline brought on by trying to get noticed and seemingly succeeding.

The next day, during our typical film study, I grew excited as I anticipated the coaches reviewing the play with us. I thought I had made a big play and looked forward to getting a little recognition by Coach Marciano in front of my teammates. As the play filled up the white screen and began to roll, a little smile formed on my face. This hopeful anticipation was soon crushed by a booming voice as Coach Marciano yelled, "Who is this?"

"That's me," I answered, raising my hand. I'm pretty sure he already knew that. He wanted me to take accountability. "Never do that again! If I see you ever do it again, you won't be here the next day." My face flushed crimson with both embarrassment and confusion. It was a stark reminder that I could be gone, my dream cut short—instantly.

Afterward, I asked the coach, "What did I do wrong?" He explained I had gotten lucky. The goal of the wedge buster is to do just that—break apart that rolling wall so they can't block anyone else. So our tacklers can make the play on the returner. Had I missed the play on the returner *and* not broken the wedge, stopping them from blocking, it could have led to a touchdown. I thought I had made a brilliant play, but I hadn't done my job. Coach understood I was giving my all—that my choice was borne from effort—but he was also teaching me a valuable lesson: *Do what you're told.*

The highlight of my whole Texans experience was the Hall of Fame game, the first preseason game of the NFL season, which we played against the New York Giants in Canton, Ohio. My dad's first NFL game with the New Orleans Saints had also been the Hall of Fame game years before. I'd never been to Canton and seen the Hall of Fame, so the significance, the legacy story it provided for our family, coursed through my veins. A come-full-circle moment for my dad and me.

My dad, who had incredible athletic ability and was a hard worker, had unfortunately squandered his football opportunities with poor decisions off the field, which hurt him and his football career. He had been the most valuable player (MVP) of the freshman team at West Virginia University (WVU). Then, he had been suspended for a campus fight and left WVU in the aftermath. He never graduated from college, but with his talent, he was picked up as a free agent and signed with the Chicago Bears and later with the New Orleans Saints. He played for the Bears minor league affiliate, the Chicago Owls, and dressed in the same locker room as the great Gale Sayers and Dick Butkus. Then he was picked up by the Saints as a wide receiver and battled it out in camp with the famous All-Pro Ken Burrough for playing time and a roster spot.

For my entire life, my dad had talked about this game—the Hall of Fame game. Then, years later in my football journey, I was introduced as a Texan at the same game. As I prepared to run out of the tunnel (it aired for Monday Night football), I spied my mom and dad in the front row, on the right-hand side, at the end of the tunnel. Tears streamed down my dad's cheeks. And I started to tear up too. I thought to myself, *I love you guys, but you need to pull it together, Dad! I need to be ready to play.*

When we locked eyes, the special moment for our family was consummated. We all knew my being there, at *that* game, was a testament to God's faithfulness—His love for us. After so many years of hearing about all of the things I couldn't do and how I wasn't good or big enough, and marrying that to all of the times my dad told me that my hard work and genetics were there so I should keep working . . . and to see the fruit of my trust in the Lord . . . I knew I was experiencing a gift from God.

> *Every good gift and every perfect gift is from above, coming down from the Father of lights, with whom there is no variation or shadow due to change* (James 1:17).

The refs called me for a clip on a punt return, and that ended up being my only measurable statistic from that night. They were right too. I had made a great hit, but I wasn't able to get my head in front, so I clipped him. Coach was irate. He removed me from the punt return team for the rest of the night. We lost the game, but the experience—the sights, sounds, and feelings—of playing in the same game as my dad years ago on Monday night football will forever be etched into my memory.

I played in a few other games, but I ended up getting released about a week before the end of preseason. With every round of cuts, a couple of assistants—we called them the "grim reapers"—would wait in the tunnel that connected our practice field with the game field. Several days before the start of the season, as we entered the tunnel, an assistant approached me and said, "Coach wants to see you. Go grab your playbook."

In an instant, I knew what was coming. My heart fluttered, and my gut turned over.

Coach Dom Capers, the Texans head coach, is a believer. We had team chapels before games, and he participated in every one. He ran a tight ship but coached fairly. My cut happened in a matter of minutes, but Coach Capers handled it professionally, leaving me feeling good about my journey. I cried in his office as he kindly explained that I had done a great job. "You gave 100 percent effort all of the time. Unfortunately, we have a lot of guys, and you weren't able to get a lot of reps. I know you didn't play safety in college. But you picked it up really fast. However, we've got a couple of other guys who we drafted this year, and we want to give them time to develop. I wish you the best." When I turned to leave, he said, "Oh, and Josh, Coach Joe Marciano wants to talk with you too."

I made my way to the special teams coordinator's office, feeling my goal of a career in the NFL evaporating again. It was a notion that did not leave me feeling lighter. My legs shuffled, but I wanted to face this disappointment head-on, as best as I could, so I stood taller and entered Coach Marciano's office.

"Josh, I want to let you know that I saw the effort you gave us. You *do* have the ability to play at this level. But we just have to make really tough decisions. Maybe we can bring you back as a practice squad guy. So stay near your phone." The next words he said encouraged me, and I'll never forget them. "If I had fifty-five guys that played like you, with the passion and effort you demonstrate, we'd win a championship." That was a special moment. I wept again. His acknowledgment of the work I had put in every second that I stepped onto the field meant more than he probably realized. He didn't have to say that. He didn't have to see me at all. And I'll be forever grateful.

> *Therefore encourage one another and build one another up, just as you are doing* (1 Thessalonians 5:11).

Everything that day stung. I'd never been cut before. Getting cut is an interesting experience, and as I said, the Texans handled it professionally on all levels.

I went down to get my stuff from my locker, but with the NFL's efficient ways, my locker had already been cleared out. My personal items were in a trash bag on the floor next to my locker. I decided not to grab my helmet, a choice I'd later regret. It was an emotional decision. *Why would I want the helmet from the team that cut me?* I had thought.

I had taken my high school helmet, my college helmet (after paying for it), and my NFL Europe helmet, which I lost later when my car was stolen. I wish I had taken my Texans helmet too.

I underwent the exit physical—a policy to protect the NFL from cut players saying they were let go because they were injured or not healthy at the time—and then, they put me in a car to the airport and gave me a plane ticket back to Orlando. I didn't get to say goodbye to most of my teammates—only my roommate, the punter. I wished him the best, and that was it.

Then, I flew back home to figure out what to do next.

RED ZONE CHECK

1. God is faithful no matter where our journeys take us—through highs and lows and everywhere between. He provides us with personal gifts, special gifts only we can understand or appreciate because He's a personal God. Think about a gift God has given you. How does it feel to be so well-known by the Creator of the universe and beyond? (Psalm 139:1–24)

2. Despite getting cut, Coach Marciano's words to me were encouraging, and I needed them at that time. Have you ever been discouraged, but then God placed someone in your life to share an uplifting word at just the right time? Did you ever thank them? Did you praise God for His provision for you? If not, consider reaching out and letting them know and take a minute to thank God. (1 Thessalonians 5:11)

Chapter 10

THE AGENT

The hope that God has provided for you is not merely a wish. Neither is it dependent on other people, possessions, or circumstances for its validity.
John C. Broger

OK, God, is this it?

It was late August 2002, and I did the only thing I knew to do. I went back to training, hoping to get another opportunity to live out my dream. I went back to substitute teaching and working out with my old high school team at Lake Highland. This time around, I had more clout than before. My football career, while not landing where I had hoped it would, had progressed. I had been a starter in NFL Europe; I'd gone to camp with the Texans. Those two things were accomplishments I could hang my helmet on, so to speak—even though I didn't take my Texans helmet with me. My agent continued to try to find me another workout or, at least, the chance for a team to pick me up for their practice squad. In the end, neither the Texans nor any other team brought me back. I called my agent periodically to check in, but he had no news. The feelings of rejection and desperation grew.

In late October, my agent called. "Josh, I think that I've done all that I can do for you. I've tried to get you workouts, and it doesn't seem like we're going to get another shot." He had taken me on as a client as a special project and because we shared the Christian faith. I knew he could only carry so many clients, and he had higher revenue-potential athletes on his plate.

I contacted another agent who was just getting started in the business, an attorney who loved sports and who was also a Christian. Matt Schultz was driven by the goal of breaking into the industry, so he agreed to represent me, saying, "Hey, we're both hungry. No one is giving us a chance. So I'll fight for you." Then, Matt made more calls on my behalf.

One thing he learned in his research while building his contacts gutted me and undermined much of the hard work I had put in over the past many years. "Josh, there is a bogus forty time out there for you. They have your official time down slower than a 4.6."

"Matt, I ran a 4.45 during the Yale pro-scout day with the Jets, Patriots, and others. The one scout showed me what he had on his clock. Also, remember . . . I ran the fastest time at Yale as a true freshman, under a 4.6, way back then!" I couldn't stop defending myself. "And I ran track the first two years at Yale. I've worked on my speed . . . I'm faster now." Desperation coursed through my veins. Official times for the forty-yard dash are crucial to NFL decision-makers.

I knew I was running consistently in the low 4.50s, high 4.40s for my forty. When I had tried out with the Toronto Argonauts, I had run a 4.45. But all that didn't matter. My stats were incorrect, and everyone saw me as a 4.6 guy. It was atrocious. The news hurt, and white-hot frustration grew in the pit of my stomach. Even though Matt fought against the erroneous information and tried to contact teams to convince them the time was bogus—that I wasn't "slow" as the time suggested—they only saw me as a white guy who played a skilled position and who'd come from Yale . . . a player who just wasn't fast enough. I had been written off.

The NFL season ended while I sat at home.

One afternoon in January 2003, I was watching TV at my parents' house. As I flipped through the channels, something grabbed my attention. It was Arena football. While it had started back in 1987, I knew little about it. I'd heard of it and had even worked out with some guys who played for the Orlando Predators—and those guys had been high-level college players—but I wasn't too familiar with it. I also knew Kurt Warner had played Arena football. When I looked him up, I saw he had turned to the Iowa Barnstormers in 1995 when no NFL team had initially picked him up, and in 1998, he had played for the same NFL Europe team as me, the Amsterdam Admirals, before earning a spot on the St. Louis Rams later that same year. The most interesting thing about seeing the sport on TV was that NBC was airing it. That meant something, I believed.

I called my new agent. "Hey, Matt, what about Arena football?"

He agreed it might be a good move, so he made a few calls. Within a week or two, I had a workout with the Chicago Rush. It was an interesting deal. They signed me for a three-day agreement to basically bring me up and have me practice, much like a working interview.

"Josh, I'm going up there with you," Matt offered. "Let's do this." His confidence and support fueled me.

I contacted Chris Barber who was an assistant coach at Lake Highland. I knew he had played Arena football for many years, and I asked him to help me prepare. I needed to understand the game because it's different from regular, eleven-man football.

Coach Barber met me at the Lake Highland field and set up some cones, showing me the size of the Arena ball field, which is only fifty yards long. Then he took me through some drills and gave me a few pointers. One major difference between the NFL and Arena was what's called "high-motion" by one of the wide receivers. That WR gets a full-speed head start at the line of scrimmage and the quarterback tries to time up the snap so the center hikes the ball just as that WR is hitting the line. It's a huge offensive advantage, part of why the Arena game is so high scoring. Coach Barber taught me how to guard against that motion, how to stay square with my hips, and more. He worked with me for a full day on the post, corner post, and post-corner-post plays.

Matt bought our plane tickets on his dime, and we flew to Chicago a few days later. I signed the three-day contract and was given a helmet and pads. My nerves fired as I mentally prepared for a game that differed from what I was used to playing. I prayed that what I had learned from Coach Barber would be enough.

In Chicago, I put on my pads for the first practice. I didn't know any of the guys, and that felt weird. Typically, in other leagues of football, you don't just join a team in mid-season, even for practices. This team had already played a few games.

During that first day, I was on the "scout team" for offense first, which meant the coaches showed me a card that told me the route to run or the coverage to play and just sent me out there to do what was on the card.

When I switched to defense, Coach Barber's time with me paid off. I was covering one of the best receivers in the league—Antonio Chatman ("AC")—a guy who would later move to the NFL and play for the Green Bay Packers and Cincinnati Bengals. He was extremely quick and did it all as the "offensive specialist" for the Rush, including returning kick-offs. He was often that high-motion wide receiver, and I was tasked with covering him.

One of the first plays where I was matched up with AC, he ran a quick out toward the sideline, which is a padded wall in Arena football. I made a hard break to his up-field shoulder. He caught the ball since the QB anticipated everything well and released the pigskin before AC even broke out of his route. But I made contact with AC just as the ball touched his hands, and I drove him into the wall. On the next play, AC lined up in the slot and ran into the backfield to gain momentum for flying back toward the line in high motion. Though this was a high-speed play, my mind processed it in slow motion.

This is my chance. This is what I worked on with Coach Barber. I'm ready for this, I thought. AC hit the line at full speed and angled toward my inside foot, "stemming" his route to take away my inside leverage. I stayed square and angled my back foot to pedal and maintain the inside position. As AC closed in on me and started to break my cushion, I anticipated a fake at the top of the route. He took two small steps to the post and then broke back out to the corner. But I didn't buy the fake, and I was right there to knock the ball away. AC smiled at me. "Nice play, rookie!" It felt more than satisfying to get even that small amount of recognition from a player like him.

I didn't shut down AC completely, but for a guy who'd never played Arena football before, I made some solid plays. I deflected several more passes and even intercepted a ball before the end of the day. During the hitting drills, I was sold out and busted my butt—as I'd always done throughout my life—and showed the coaches that I loved contact and wasn't afraid to tackle anybody.

I made it through the three days without getting cut. At the end of my mini-contract, the coaches told me the good news. "Josh, we want to sign you for the rest of the season." Relief flooded my bloodstream. I had done it. *No, God paved the way for me.* I silently thanked Him.

Signing with the Rush was a huge blessing that I whole-heartedly attributed to God, Matt, and my hard work, in that order. I've always

RED ZONE CHECK

1. Has anyone ever fought for you, especially if you were tired of fighting for yourself? Have you had someone stand up for you, encouraging you, when everyone else seemed to have given up on you? What did that kind of support mean to you? What was the outcome? (Deuteronomy 3:22)

2. Have you ever prepared for a moment in life and been ready to perform when that moment came? The work that you put in had prepared you to act, almost by instinct, when the moment arrived? Has that ever happened spiritually? Where the time in God's Word, or the preparation garnered from a previous trial and how God grew you, had given you just what you needed to stand in that moment? (Ephesians 6:13)

Chapter 11

THE TWO FISH

Pray as though everything depended on God.
Work as though everything depended on you.
Augustine

As I walked back into the Rush locker room on Monday of the following week, memories of when I entered that bus for my first high school football camp plagued my mind. Just like back then, I didn't know my new teammates very well. These guys were at the height of their season, many of them Arena League veterans, and some were All-League Players. Not only did I not know the guys well, I was still studying the sport. I had much to learn.

The Chicago Rush had rented out a few units in one particular apartment complex for team members to stay (paid for by the team), which I was relieved to discover. I wouldn't have to find my own place or figure out how to pay for it.

Walking into that first week, I flashed back to the words from the Texans' coaches when they released me from the team, that my effort was unlike any of the other players, and they had appreciated it more than I knew. I took on that same mentality, now playing for the Chicago Rush. I wanted to earn my way onto the field, to become a starter. I wanted to go from barely knowing the game at all to fighting for a spot . . . and succeeding . . . in just a few short weeks. A tall order, for sure.

The lesson I had learned and relearned throughout my life was now going to apply to this new situation, and it was this: There are only a few things we can control in our lives; they are our *effort* and our *attitude*. I never wanted it to be said that the reason I didn't get somewhere was because I didn't give it everything I had. My parents and teachers, coaches and others had all trained me to do everything for God's glory.

Whatever you do, work heartily, as for the Lord and not for men (Colossians 3:23).

Every opportunity that presented itself on the field, I showed the coaches something. During kick-offs, on a field half the length of the NFL field, the ball bounces off of nets hanging above the turf. This adds a little time to the play because the returner has to turn his back to the defense to catch the ball. After catching the ball, in the following split second, the returner must turn back around and read his blocks quickly to earn any forward movement.

My goal was to get down the field so fast that I would beat the ball down there. I would run hard enough to get to the returner before he would even turn around so I could tackle him immediately and make the play.

In Arena football, there are two returners, and the goal of the one who doesn't get the ball is to block what's called, "the most dangerous man." I wanted to be that dangerous man on the field. I wanted to blow past that second returner. On our team, his name was Damien Porter, or DP.

DP was an Arena League veteran. And in practice, with this strategy of mine in full motion, the coaches turned to DP with their hands in the air. "What's going on?" they shouted at him. I was running by my blocker and then running right through DP, trying to get to the returner with the ball. Crazy White had re-emerged and was making an appearance in Arena football.

What I didn't realize was that each week, the team named a "Practice Player of the Week." That first full week on the team, I was honored with the title. And that title came with a bunch of money—cash, actually. Throughout the week, the coaches and staff would fine players for various things, such as being late to meetings, breaking curfew, and uniform violations, among other things. They discovered that hitting adults in the pocketbook was a much more effective way to curb poor behavior than making them run or do up-downs. The team collected the fines into one large pool of money, which they gave to the Practice Player of the Week.

Later, when I counted the money, I realized I had nearly doubled my normal weekly salary. I was making practice squad money, well below $35,000 per year. So this cash reward mattered to me. A lot. And make no mistake: It wasn't just the cash but the recognition that mattered. Elation filled me, and I called my parents to let them know about my growing success.

This recognition fired me up, and a new goal emerged. I wanted to win this pot of money every week until they moved me to the active roster. There were seven weeks left in the season. My self-imposed deadline loomed.

After the first couple of weeks of pounding hard, running through DP at full speed, and winning the cash, DP and I had an encounter. I arrived at the practice facility early, and he was there. I don't know if he was waiting for me or what, but it was just him and me. He approached me with a furrowed brow.

"Hey, man. Can you chill on kick-off? Dial it down a little? Man, I ain't trying to feel this [explicative] today."

I calmly walked over to him and looked him in the eyes. "I can't, man. I haven't been in the league. I'm new. I haven't done what you've done. I've been cut once from the Texans, and I never want to get cut again. I want to play. There's no tomorrow for me. If I get cut, it's over. I have to give it everything I have and give it at that level every day. It's nothing personal, man. I want to be here because I just love this game."

DP paused and thought about my words. "I respect you, man."

He shook my hand. In the next few weeks, when we slammed into each other on kickoff, he gave me a sly smile. He started hitting me back harder—my consistent effort made DP step up his practice intensity. Eventually, he started giving me a pro tip here and there. I appreciated that because I knew I had earned his respect and the respect of others.

I accomplished half of my goals that season. I won the Practice Player of the Week every week until the final game ended. However, I hadn't yet been called up to active playing status.

At the end of the season, the coaches called me to their offices. I remembered the Texans training camp experience of being called to the offices to be cut from the team. Despite my fear, I squared my shoulders as I went to speak to the Chicago Rush coaches, controlling the tremors in my nervous body.

In his office, the head coach, Mike Hohensee, looked me in the eyes and offered me a contract for the following year. I exhaled a long breath and internally celebrated. Outwardly, I thanked him and immediately signed the contract. The flashback of getting cut receded into my long-term memory bank as I looked ahead, grateful for this newly created memory to offset the one in the Texans' coaches' offices. My future seemed bright.

To know I had a place to come back to next year was one of the most rewarding feelings I'd ever experienced. They wanted *me*. With my signature, I had every intention of earning that starting spot and getting on that active roster. I left his office filled with gratitude.

I spent the off-season in Boca Raton, Florida at Chris Carter's FAST Program, a place I had gone to train at various times in my football career. Pro athletes from all levels attend this program, and when I arrived, I saw many notable players, including Randy Moss, Desmond Howard, Daunte Culpepper, and Qadry "The Missile" Ismail. I intuitively knew this program would help me reach my goal—to start on the Chicago Rush the next year. For the team's confidence in me, I hoped to reward their faith by training harder and becoming better.

My dad had always encouraged me with one simple truth, one I still believe is true. When you seek people who are better than you, you will grow. My dad had taught me: Don't be the big fish in a little pond because that's not the best measuring stick to reach your best. Go be a little fish in the big pond because it will help you determine where your deficiencies are so you can become better. We all have a tendency to do the minimum amount needed for success, and then we become comfortable. But when we dare enough to enter the big pond, our weaknesses and what we need to work on emerge, and we discover where we're falling short. The fact is, we can only change what we allow ourselves to see.

Make no mistake. It's a hard pill to swallow when you discover where you lack in skill or ability. But it's a decision you make for your personal (even spiritual) development. When others are bigger, stronger, faster, or even more talented, you have two choices. You can either quit or you can respond and say, "I know I can work to get myself to that level." A growth mindset and a positive mentality are critical to reaching your full potential. I was taught to choose to see these things and seek out the challenge.

At Chris Carter's FAST Program, the level of talent and competitiveness pushed me to grow exponentially. On one occasion, I had the privilege of being paired with Desmond Howard in a pro agility drill where we had to run against each other during fifteen mini races, keeping score during the drill. Desmond Howard won a Heisman Trophy and a Super Bowl MVP with the Green Bay Packers. I was never the player that Desmond proved to be. But I did beat him eight times out of the fifteen in these pro agility races. Maybe he didn't give his all in some of them, but on that day, I beat him for a tiny majority. The reason I'm sharing this story is that other guys, other players, were cheering us on and poking fun at him, all while noticing my effort. That built my confidence because facing these elite players was intimidating. Going head to head against an athlete the caliber of Desmond Howard reminded me I was capable of playing at the highest level.

If we don't believe it ourselves, no one can believe it for us.

Another time, Qadry Ismail, a wide receiver with the Baltimore Ravens, was looking for someone to throw the ball around with and execute one-on-ones. No one was around but me. I boldly stepped up. "Hey, I'll go with you. I'd love to do it."

Twenty minutes later, we were on the field, and I had the opportunity to go against Qadry. Though he was trying to beat me and win the rep, he was also giving me tips. They were pointers about how to use my other hand (or foot). He'd say to me, "When I do this move, here's how you counter it . . . when I lean in and push off, here's how you get a little grab and absorb the energy without holding." This time was priceless.

That day against Qadry, I won some reps and improved because I surrounded myself with greatness, with big fish. The FAST Program continued to bolster my abilities, and I hoped it was enough to compete at any level, particularly in the Arena League.

One of the best things the FAST Program ever provided me was my friend and brother for life, Ivery Gaskins. The first summer I challenged myself to train with these incredible athletes was 2000—right before my senior year at Yale. I came in one afternoon, frustrated because a University of Florida wide receiver who was organizing the on-field throwing activities kept failing to let me know when they were meeting. It happened often enough (and despite repeated reminders) that it became clear to me he was purposely leaving me out. I'm not a mind reader, but there were elements of our interactions that led me to think his attitude toward me was racially motivated. So I felt hurt and ostracized. It brought back those feelings of being left out that I had experienced back at Lake Highland Prep. As I walked into the FAST facility to talk to the training staff about the incident, I saw this massive, ripped, shirtless athlete running on the super treadmill. He heard me talking to the staff and veered toward me after his workout to introduce himself.

"Hi. My name is Ivery Gaskins," he said as he reached out his hand to give me a firm handshake.

I asked him what position he played, though I assumed he was a linebacker, given his build.

"I play wide receiver."

I was shocked. This guy was built like a Greek god. Imagine Terrel Owens but maybe an inch shorter.

I asked, "How much do you bench?"

He replied with genuine humility, "Oh, I try not to bench too much; it makes my chest too big." I shook my head. I thought for a second that he was kidding. But as I looked at his facial expression, I realized he wasn't joking, nor was he being cocky. To this day, this is just the wild genetics he has—his body's response to training is so robust that he gains mass very quickly. He could easily be a professional body builder if he wanted to be.

Ivery offered to throw with me anytime I wanted to get some work in. I got his number to text him, and we met at the field just a couple of hours later for the first of what would be many epic training sessions to come. He was on a scholarship at the University of Central Florida at the time. So we got together every time I was back home in Orlando—over school breaks and the summer—to push each other, including that fateful evening when I tore my hamstring while racing him in those 150 meters before my Tampa Bay Buccaneers tryout.

Besides that unfortunate injury, training with IG always made me better. He gave me that perfect mix of a brother who loves and supports you, but who also pushes you in love and challenges you to be your better. That challenge wasn't just physical, it was spiritual as well. IG is a brother in Christ and a man I truly respect and admire in terms of his walk and the integrity with which he lives his life. Our training battles were all-out wars. We would go *mano y mano* in one-on-ones similar to what I described with Qadry Ismail, but amp up the physicality a few notches.

Ivery always wanted to get in my head to start; he would look in at whatever QB was throwing the ball and tap the top of his head. This is a universal symbol that you're going deep. Whether he went deep or not, IG always started this way. It's mildly disrespectful because what he's really saying is, "I'm going deep, I'm letting you know and you still can't stop me." If he wanted to get me fired up, he got his wish. I would be hyper-aggressive at the line of scrimmage, trying to jam him or get my hands on him and disrupt his route.

During one of these battles, his shirt ripped as I made contact at the line.

He said, "See, you have to hold me to stop me."

The next rep, I purposefully grabbed him and ripped his shirt clean off.

"Put another shirt on, and I'll rip that one off too!" I said as I spiked what was left of his tattered shirt on the ground.

As intense as these workouts were, it was still all in love. We never reached the point of an altercation and always put our arms around each other at the end and encouraged one another. Rarely in life do we ever truly accomplish anything on our own. Even if we feel we may have been self-made or have defied the odds, often there are people working behind the scenes in life that made it possible for us to achieve. During almost all of my training stints at FAST, I stayed with my mom's West Virginia childhood friend, Karleen O'Brien, who treated me like a son. She had relocated to southern Florida years before and only lived thirty minutes away from Ft. Lauderdale. She graciously opened her home and guest room for me. Karleen was so supportive that she and another family friend, Barbara Mills, flew all the way to Amsterdam to watch me play in NFL Europe. I saw God's hand continuing to place people like this on my journey, every step of the way. From Coach Borcky at LHP to my football Bible Study brothers at Yale, and from Blaine and Kevin and Ivery to many more—God was always working, and He was always faithful.

> *As iron sharpens iron, so one man sharpens another* (Proverb 27:17).

Not every person is blessed enough to find a brother from another mother like IG in life. But if you ever do, praise God for it. IG sharpened me in every sense of the word.

I left FAST in January 2004 to head back to Illinois, feeling physically and mentally ready to win the job with the Chicago Rush.

RED ZONE CHECK

1. Have you ever been pressured to be less than what you could be? Has peer pressure ever convinced you to settle? If so, do you regret it? Is there a way to create a second chance for yourself or get back what you lost when you gave in to someone else's limiting expectations or boundaries for you? (Proverbs 12:5)

2. Are you a big fish in a little pond or a little fish in a big pond? What are the benefits of both? If you're a big fish in a little pond, why might you think about becoming a little fish and step outside of your comfort zone? In what areas could you do this today? (2 Corinthians 4:18)

3. Has God placed supportive people in your path that have helped you take steps along your journey? Who are they? How have they helped you? Can you see how pivotal they were to your life? Write their names down, and if you're willing, consider offering up some prayers of thanksgiving for their role in your life. (Galatians 6:2)

Chapter 12

THE WATERSHED

Our lives consist of moments. Stitched together like the seams on a coat, these moments cloak us in awareness and possibility.
Gari Meacham

In our lives, we'll reach watershed moments, dividing points from which things will never be the same.

When I returned to Chicago and arrived in the team apartments, I was matched with a few new roommates. A mutual friend connected me with another new player, Sam Clemons, who came into The Rush's training camp after playing quarterback for the Dallas Cowboys. Sam lived in the same apartment complex but was in a different building.

I knew from our mutual friend Sam was a Christian. We'd both been told we'd likely become good friends. And true to that prediction, Sam and I quickly formed a friendship, born from a common drive to be better football players and Christian men. Sam and I made a conscious decision to out-work everybody else. We knew we needed to go above and beyond what was expected to earn our starting spots.

Early on those Chicago-cold mornings, well before anyone else was awake, Sam and I showed up. He would throw, and I ran routes, and then we would watch extra film before practice started. It was so cold in the months of January and February that our Gatorade would freeze if we left the bottles in our cars overnight. Many times, we took his car to the practice arena because the doors on my car would freeze shut. Sam's SUV sported heated seats, which made the freezing cold rides much more bearable once I hopped into his car. No matter what obstacle we faced—frozen locks or tired bodies or something else—we got to practice early because we were dedicated to our goals.

Our teammates worked hard on the field, but many other players' lifestyles—particularly my roommates'—were a bit different off the field. My apartment often smelled like weed, and these guys drank at night, even during training camp. There was one super-talented guy who played the same position as me, and through the first several weeks and the first rounds of cuts, it became clear: The two-way active roster spot would likely come down to him and me.

Since we were roommates, there was a bit of a professional rivalry. His friends, who were our other roommates, were some of the stars on the team. It seemed obvious they wanted him to make the team over me by the way they would react in practice when he made a play versus when I did. The living situation was awkward. When I came in and out of the house, conversations would go quiet. The guys were civil, but there was often tension hanging in the air. It brought back memories of my freshman year at Lake Highland and the way those players treated me at camp. I felt like an outsider again—not welcome into the inner circle.

Despite their inclinations, my extra effort, focus and tenacity secured me the roster spot. Thank goodness I had Sam.

Sam had a roommate who frequently spent time over at my place. And when he returned to Sam's apartment at all hours of the night, sometimes arguing on the phone, he'd wake up Sam. So Sam and I came up with the idea that maybe this guy and I could switch apartments. I knew it would be good for me to get away from what was happening in my apartment and into Sam's, where we could both focus on football and our faith.

I approached Sam's roommate and asked if he'd be willing to trade. "You're spending more time at my place, and vice versa. What do you think?"

He agreed. That paved the way for me to build an even stronger relationship with the Christian brother I'd found in Sam. Together, we focused on becoming starting players and accountability partners in Christ.

Before our third game, when the team was preparing to travel east to take on the New York Dragons, the coaches asked me to travel too. I knew I'd finally earned my first opportunity to play in a game.

The New York Dragons' quarterback, Aaron Garcia, was an All-League player. He held Arena League records with 104 touchdown passes in a season and eleven in a single game. It was quite a challenging set-up for my first professional arena game experience. Early in the second quarter, Coach Hohensee called my number, and I entered the game at the corner position. I appreciated the moment and all that came with it. My senses were on high alert as I took in the field, the sounds, and our opponents. Garcia, being the savvy veteran he was, took aim at me immediately. He knew he had a rookie out there on an island at corner, and he quickly went to work. He surgically completed a couple of short passes—a slant and a quick out in front of me. The Dragons moved the ball right down the field and into scoring position at our fifteen-yard line. On the next play, the wide receiver ran a post corner (a double-move on me). Had it not been for the double-move, I'd have had him dead to rights. I was in a good position, with inside leverage, making my stand at the goal line, wedged between the receiver and the ball. But when he made the double-move and cut back outside, he swam over me with his right arm as he broke free into the back right corner of the end zone. Garcia lofted a perfect touch ball that reached the receiver's outstretched arms right before he hit the wall, and they scored the touchdown. That was not the way I wanted to start my first drive in the Arena League.

I'd bounced back from rough plays before and was determined to redeem myself. In the next series, they threw a slant on the other side of the field, and the receiver cut toward my side. I thought, *I've got this.* I was going to blow him up because he was looking downfield and didn't even see me. Just as I launched my whole body toward him, the receiver made a hard stop, then he dodged to the right. I caught him with only my left arm. With all of my momentum going one way, and him going in the opposite direction, I hung on for dear life. That's when I felt a severe *Pop!* in my left chest area. The guy ran for another five yards but was tackled by one of my teammates.

When I hopped up, I felt it. On my gosh, it burned. The pain stretched from my chest to my arm. I went back to my position, but my extremity felt like it was hanging off my shoulder. I tried to lift my arm and press it forward, in a blocking motion, but it wouldn't move. *Something is wrong,* I thought, but I didn't know what it was. The Dragons scored on us in the next couple of plays, and then I had to stay on the field for the kick-off return. I tried to work my body in front of people, but I had become a one-armed blocker.

When halftime arrived and we went into the locker room, I headed over to the trainer. I removed my pads, and after some various strength tests, he said, "You're done," and he took my pads. My heart ached knowing my first Arena League action ended the same day it began and with a serious injury. Anguish forced its way back into my mind and soul.

When we returned to Chicago, I underwent an MRI, which showed a torn pectoralis muscle. The team doctors and surgeon told me an operation was the only answer. It had been a few days, and the swelling had not relented. My upper arm, the area around the biceps, was completely black with bruises.

In the days it took to get the results of the MRI, I tried to do things with my arm. It hurt, but I could move it. I even went to the gym while all of my teammates, my only friends in Chicago, were at practice. I had to do something. So I worked out the other parts of my body and kept trying things with my arm.

I knew if I had surgery and went on the injured reserve, I'd be out for the rest of the year. Not only that, I'd have to wear a sling on my arm, effectively restricted from any movement for several weeks before I could even start rehab. I didn't want to be immobile for a month; I knew my season would be over, and I feared what that would mean for my future. It was a weighty decision, so I asked for a second opinion.

After his exam, the second surgeon said, "Josh, it's up to you. I could operate. I could not operate. Your muscle has torn away from the tendon, which is still attached to the bone. If your tendon had been ripped off, I'd have to re-anchor it in surgery. And it's usually a very successful surgery. But because your muscle was torn away from the tendon, there's no guarantee that if I stretched it back and tried to sow it to the tendon, it'd be strong again. In fact, the likelihood of a repeat tear would be pretty high. You're already able to do some things. You're not strong, but you're showing signs of improvement. I recommend you try to rehab it for the next several weeks. See what you can get out of it. We can still do surgery later if needed."

That made sense to me, and I chose that route and started the rehab process. It was painstakingly slow. Painful. And depressing. I hated not being able to play. Emotionally and mentally, I was thrust right back into the situation I had been when I had graduated from college and torn my hamstring. Spiritually and psychologically, I receded, wondering who I was without football. That slide backward, caused by the injury and some other events happening around me, forced me into the most contemplative period of my life, one filled with self-evaluation the likes of which I had never truly done before.

I had entered one of life's watershed moments.

A few weeks had gone by, but it was still early in my recovery. The team had agreed to keep me on injured reserve and allow me the chance to work on things without surgery, even though it was against the team doc's advice. They told me I could come off of the injured reserve list if I got healthy, so I attended the practices, listening from the sidelines, and stayed engaged. Afterward, I would go to the gym to do my rehab.

A "bye week," when the team had no game, arrived, and the coaches gave us a long weekend, so I flew home to Florida to be with my family. My brother, Jacob, who was the second youngest of the seven kids in our family also came home that weekend. He was eight years my senior, so I truly was the baby of all of my siblings. Jacob once told me, "I was the baby until you stole it!" and we both laughed.

Jacob had fallen into substance abuse, starting with alcohol and later including drugs, earlier in our lives. He had been in and out of rehab and jail, including a time on house arrest when I was a senior in high school.

Jacob had been attending a particular rehabilitation program for nearly two years, The Phoenix House—which he had asked to be sentenced to at his last court hearing for drug possession—and he had been progressing to the point where he could come home for occasional weekend visits. He had worked to make amends, written us letters, and when he was allowed visitors, I had gone to see him a handful of times. He was reaching the phase where he'd soon get out on his own, find an apartment, secure a job outside of the program, and essentially get his life back. He had been clean for a long time.

Standing on the front porch next to our mom, I watched as Jacob stepped out of the car with both hands behind his back. When he reached us, he pulled his right hand out and offered a single rose to my mom. (How sweet, right?) "Oh, thank you, honey!" she said as she gave him a kiss. Then, Jacob pulled his other arm from behind, which held a bag of laundry.

"Mom, I love you!" he said with a laugh. Mom laughed too, and of course, she took the bag. I think her relief and gratitude far outweighed the inconvenience of doing his laundry. She loved Jacob, and it was, by all accounts, one simple act of service to show that love.

Jacob and I hung out that Friday evening. We had missed each other and wanted to bridge the gap our physical distance and his addiction had caused over the years. And that Friday held a couple of mini-adventures for us to build memories. We went to our brother Jerry's house to celebrate our nephew Tyler's birthday. Afterward, at a gas station, we found what looked like a stray Border Collie-Australian Shepherd mix running around the parking lot. It was friendly and had a collar, so Jacob and I took on the challenge of catching it. The name tag read "Noelle." We brought Noelle to our parents' house and put her on the back deck, then called the owners, who said they'd pick her up the next morning. We felt good about helping.

That night, Jacob and I met up with some of my friends in Orlando, but there was a problem: Jacob had no clothes appropriate for "going out."

"You can borrow my stuff," I offered.

So he sets himself to getting ready. I'd given him one of my shirts, but I saw he had nothing to style his hair with. A sweet brotherly moment ensued. I put some gel in my hand and helped him fix his hair.

Jacob made a classic quip: "Tell Ford if they need any overweight, slightly balding models. I'm their guy." (I had been signed by the Ford Agency to do some modeling during my first Arena League season in Chicago.) Jacob had a knack for well-timed, often self-deprecating humor that always lightened the mood. The relational gap between us seemed to close, as if it hadn't ever been there at all. It was as if we'd been close for all those missed years, and we had a great time that night out in the city.

The following day, Saturday, we ate lunch together before he left. He wanted to visit his son Trevor and his daughter, Jordan, later that day. This weekend home from rehab allowed him to see Jordan, which I know he treasured. Jacob loved being a dad, and his children had given him a renewed focus and drive to get clean. I gave him a long hug, and we told one another we loved each other.

"I'm proud of you," he said to me as he turned to leave. My heart swelled. And then he was gone.

I flew back to Chicago on Sunday. Late that night, around 1:00 a.m., my phone rang. When I answered, I heard this strange sound, hard to distinguish, in the background—a whaling-type of noise. At first, I wasn't sure if it was even human. I soon learned it was my mom, emitting a despair I cannot describe. My dad's voice came across the phone. "Son, Jacob's not breathing. Please pray!" Then he hung up.

What? Confusion and terror streaked through me, and I fell to my knees. I called and texted my other brothers, trying to get a hold of anyone who could give me more information. After several minutes, I finally reached my oldest brother, Jerry, who explained that Jacob had overdosed on drugs and was unconscious. He was taken to the hospital where they would continue to work on him.

My world narrowed, and all I could do was sit in shock. Forty-five minutes later, I received the confirmation no one ever wants to get. Jacob had passed away. I wept—bitterly—calling out to the Lord. I didn't understand. Agony rushed through me, and in my sobbing, I only knew one thing: *I needed to get home.*

I had never been through anything like this before. Both of my grandfathers had passed away when I was young. And my paternal grandmother, affectionately known as Maam, had gone home to be with Jesus when I was a freshman in college. But I'd never lost anyone like this before. A brother—someone I had just bonded with in the days before . . . even hours before. He was only thirty-two years old.

Uber and Lyft didn't exist, so I knocked on Sam's bedroom door. Through my tears, I explained my brother had just died, and I needed to get to the airport. Sam was there for me, grabbing his keys in a matter of seconds.

Around 3:00 a.m., I was scouring ticket counters at the airport and found a flight back to Florida for that Monday morning. Little did I know, this catastrophe would become another watershed moment, trumping the injury to my chest muscle.

I spoke at my brother's funeral service. It was an easy choice to do so; I wanted to honor him. I wanted to lift him up and ensure people knew that yes, he was troubled; he had battled addiction and lost, but his life was worthy of so much more. He had brought joy to people's lives. Jacob was really good at being in the moment. He knew how to enjoy what *and who* was right in front of him—as opposed to me, who was always thinking about the future and what I was trying to achieve. Jacob knew how to connect with people well, focusing on them, making them feel seen and loved. So much so, the rehab program brought a busload of people to his funeral, those who Jacob had been friends with and even just acquaintances with in the program.

Also at the funeral, my family pastor, Mark Matheson, gave a gospel presentation, giving people the opportunity to accept Jesus Christ into their lives as their Savior. Pastor Mark offered everyone in attendance, including Jacob's friends from the Phoenix House, the gift of salvation. By the grace of God, several of those young men made that life-changing decision that day.

In the coming days, I thought, *If Jacob's life and death led to others spending eternity in Heaven, in eternal fellowship with Jesus, then can*

I say it was worth it? While the thought seemed guilt-worthy, I felt a resounding *yes* in my soul.

> *Even if I am to be poured out as a drink offering upon the sacrificial offering of your faith, I am glad and rejoice with you all* (Philippians 2:17).

I communicated a bit with Sam and my coaches with the Chicago Rush while I was gone. I apologized for leaving so quickly after returning from our long weekend away. They understood and said, "Hey, it's okay. Keep us in the loop and let us know what we can do. Come back when you're ready."

In the hours, days, and weeks after Jacob's death, a new perspective filled my mind, invading my thoughts. I realized that no one is guaranteed tomorrow. Jacob, my beloved brother, obviously had issues, but any of us could be gone with our next breath. We could have an accident, an undetected heart problem, or something else. No one is promised another day.

This new perspective took up more space in my heart and brain with each passing day, and I asked myself hard questions. Questions, such as:

What is my life really about?

What am I doing?

What is my purpose here on earth?

What's most important?

And with those questions, my focus shifted. My mindset underwent a reset. As I returned to Chicago and evaluated my place, my purpose, in this world, the watershed moment of my brother's sudden death became a watershed *season* for me.

RED ZONE CHECK

1. Have you ever had to make a tough decision against the advice of a professional or a trusted mentor? How did it turn out? I haven't finished my story about my torn pec muscle yet, but what are your thoughts on my decision to try to rehabilitate it without surgery? Was it wise to get a second opinion? How do you discern the right way to go when the answer seems unclear? Will you bring God into that process? (Proverbs 14:8, 1 Corinthians 3:19)

2. I realize this chapter includes one of the traumatic parts of my story. It was difficult to write this chapter. Loss and grief are hard things. Have you ever lost someone close to you? How did you find comfort in the middle of your grief? (1 Thessalonians 4:13)

3. Has loss helped you reevaluate your humanity, your life and death journey, or the brevity of our time on Earth? What do you think your primary purpose is in this world? Have you asked God to reveal His purpose for your life? Spend some time asking God to guide and direct you to His will for your life. Write what He reveals to you. (James 4:14)

Chapter 13

THE MESSAGE

I live in the faith that there is a Presence and Power greater than I am that nurtures and supports me in ways I could not even imagine.
Ernest Holmes

I don't want to understate the time I spent with Jacob before he lost his life in that accidental overdose. It was truly a special time for both of us, the best time we'd shared in years. When people are under the influence of an addiction , they aren't the best—or even a true—version of themselves. The addiction dominates and controls people. They become slaves to the need for the drug. For years, I saw only glimpses of my brother; he would slide in and out as the drive to meet the craving and avoid the sickness of withdrawal took control.

That we had that Friday night and Saturday lunchtime together while he was sober, with no other agenda except to enjoy each other was an absolute gift from God. When I had left for Chicago, Jacob had spent that last Sunday of his life with my parents, picking up furniture for his new apartment, which was going to be located off campus from his rehab program. That entire weekend, Jacob felt excited and full of joy.

On Sunday evening, he made a decision that would ultimately end in his tragic death. Jacob went out with some friends from his past. Now, every professional in any kind of addiction program will tell you not to spend time with the people you had surrounded yourself with when you were acting out. Addicts shouldn't hang out with those who are still engaging in the old, destructive behaviors, shouldn't risk putting themselves back into the tempting situations—perhaps ever.

Well, these "friends" ended up offering Jacob drugs. He tried the same dose of heroine that he hadn't used in nearly two years, and his body couldn't handle it. We were told that within a matter of minutes after taking it, his respiratory system started to shut down.

Jacob was in the guest bathroom when my mom woke up in the middle of the night. She shot up in bed and knew something was wrong. "Where's Jacob?" she asked my dad. *She just knew.*

Both of my parents looked at the clock, which glowed with the numbers 4:44. My mom slipped out of bed and noticed the guest bathroom light was on, but the door was locked. She knocked. "Jacob? Is something wrong?"

There was no response. After a few more knocks and several long seconds, she realized he wasn't going to respond, so she grabbed my dad, who jimmied the door open. They found Jacob sprawled on the floor, passed out, and his skin an eerie shade of blue. My dad pulled him into the hallway and started CPR. My mom called 911, while my dad worked on him until the ambulance arrived. And when the paramedics took over, that's when my dad called me and told me to pray.

When I sit and consider what it must have been like for my dad, trying to resuscitate Jacob, my eyes well up. No parent should have to go through that.

My mom was hysterical with grief, but when the police arrived, they pulled my parents aside and began questioning them, then separated them. My parents thought it was strange . . . if not disrespectful. They feared for their son's life—were hysterical even. Why separate them?

They'd soon discover the reason for the police officers' actions. After being separated and interrogated by the police, they quickly dressed and hopped in their car to follow the ambulance to the hospital. My oldest brother, Jerry Michael, met them there and tried to steady them as they watched the doctors and nurses work on Jacob. My mom saw a clock outside the room across the hall that flashed 2:10 a.m. She asked the police officer stationed in the hallway what time the emergency call had come in.

"12:56 a.m.," the officer responded.

Not nearly five o'clock. When my parents were initially questioned, they had both told the authorities the time they saw was 4:44, so the police separated them, believing my parents were potentially high on drugs too.

When I arrived in Florida for Jacob's service, my parents told me this part of the story. We started praying about it because it was so bizarre—that *both* of them, with certainty, saw the clock, and it had said 4:44. We wondered if there was a message in it. So I opened the Bible to look.

Rather quickly, I felt led to the book of Psalms. I looked for Psalm 4:44, but there is no such verse. I flipped to Psalm 44:4 and read:

> *You are my King, O God; ordain deliverance for Jacob!*

Our hearts leaped within our chests. We firmly believe the message was for our family, a comforting promise from God to carry with us in our grief. Obviously, that specific verse is talking about Israel and refers to the Jacob of the Bible. But it's also about God being the deliverer, the rescuer of His people. Not because of their goodness or because they earned it, but because He is a faithful God and He is Good. Comfort embraced us like a warm blanket as this Scripture gave us the assurance that our Jacob was safe in the arms of Jesus. *Deliverance for Jacob!*

My mom had shot up in bed that awful night though there'd been no sound. As I said above, she just knew something was wrong with Jacob. Moms always seem to know, much like twins who have a special sense of one another. My family believes that was when Jacob was passing from this earth to his heavenly home. We think Mom was awakened by a presence—an angel, or God, or perhaps Jacob's spirit on its way to heaven. And then she and my dad looked at the clock. *4:44. I've got him.*

We trust God was telling us, "He's with me now." Of course, we'll always wonder about these kinds of things on this side of Heaven. We were not the first family to experience other-worldly phenomena, and I doubt we were the last. But God, in His love for us, comforted us with those red numbers that had shone through the darkness.

My brother did not commit suicide. He had been filled with hope and joy that weekend, excited to be transitioning out of the rehab center soon and get his own place. He was ready to move on and spend time with his kids and our family. He did not have the demeanor of someone in desperation; there was no note, no nothing. He had made a mistake, and he lost his physical life for it.

God knew what was coming long before it happened. In His unending love, first, God gave us the gift of a wonderful weekend with Jacob, and second, He gave us the gift of this message: 4:44.

You can trust Me.

Jacob is with Me.

You can rest easy.

It was such a comfort to us.

When I returned to Chicago, my mind was still reeling with thoughts of *purpose*. I was still injured, and I quietly settled back into the routine of attending part of practice and then going to the gym for rehab. This kept me somewhat separated from the team, but Sam remained a good friend. On the outside, I wanted to play again soon. Inside, something was gnawing at me.

In the Arena League, there were guys in their mid- to late-thirties, and it was clear they were nearing the end of their careers. Their bodies had been beaten up from the years of playing on the old-school Astro-Turf. Most of these fields were laid in basketball and hockey arenas. The Chicago Rush practiced on an indoor soccer turf that felt like carpet laid on top of cement. It was fast but not forgiving. After less than two seasons on that surface, even my body hurt; I experienced achiness and pain in my ankles, knees, and back that I'd never felt before. And I was only in my mid-twenties. It just didn't feel good.

With many of these older players, it seemed they were hanging onto their careers because they didn't know what else to do. They didn't have any other purpose but to play football. I didn't want that to be me. My dream had been to play in the NFL. I was playing Arena football because I loved the game, and I hoped this would lead to another shot in the NFL. The Arena League was never my ultimate goal, and it just wasn't the same game.

Once I started evaluating life after Jacob's death and understood how anyone's life could end prematurely—and no one knows when—I thought about my purpose. I knew my football career could be done in a second with this injury or the next one, and I realized that was what was gnawing at me. As I thought about what I wanted people to say about my career—about my life and how I lived it—when it was all said and done, a new understanding washed over me.

I believe Jacob's life mattered. I saw the young men in his rehab program at his funeral, some of them giving their lives to Jesus, and knowing at the core of my soul that he didn't die in vain. I wanted to know my life would affect others too.

It was during this time that the movie *Passion of Christ* was released in theaters. Millions watched it. When I saw it, I thought, *Oh my gosh, millions have been exposed to the truth of Christ,* and my next thought was that *my brother's story still matters*. It will always matter.

Drugs were wreaking havoc on our society. (They still are.) The particular drug, heroine, that killed Jacob is a scourge, taking out hundreds of thousands of people and destroying families—including good Christian families like mine—creating strongholds over people and eventually killing them. If not physically, certainly emotionally and spiritually.

My insides screamed, "We have to do something about this!" But I didn't know what that something was.

I had gotten into modeling and a bit of acting around the same time I started Arena football. At the end of my first season with the Chicago Rush, I was hanging out at the mall when a scout for the Ford Modeling agency in Chicago approached me. They had brought me in and done a photoshoot—test pictures. Afterward, they gave me a contract and then sent me on several local castings, but it was hard to make that work with my training and football schedule.

During the off-season, they asked me if I was willing to do some modeling and go to castings down in Florida. I said sure and met with some agents in Miami. Soon after, I was signed by Irene Marie Models and Talent Agency through the recommendation of Ford Modeling in Chicago. Miami was only forty minutes from Boca Raton, where I was still training hard at the Chris Carter FAST program.

A friend of mine, Annie Greely, submitted an application on my behalf to appear on the reality TV show, *The Bachelorette*. After the psychological testing, bloodwork, on-camera test, and the other things they do to weed out people that wouldn't be a good fit for their show, I was chosen. A few days before flying out to Los Angeles to shoot the show in October, I asked the producers where I'd be able to train for my next football season in January.

"Oh, we have a room at the house with some dumbbells and a StairMaster."

What? "Is there a way to leave the house and go to a gym or something?" I asked. They told me it wasn't possible to go off-site. "Look, I'm a pro football player, and I need to train harder than what a few dumbbells can offer me. If I'm not in the best shape possible, I could be cut from the team. A room in the house with a few weights and a StairMaster just isn't enough . . . I guess I'm out."

I had booked a couple of little commercials the year before, and my brother, Conard, who lived in Los Angeles, was trying to convince me to go out there and live with him.

As I'm sifting through all of this—my brother's life and death, my purpose here on earth, the impact the *Passion of the Christ* was making, my modeling and acting mini-career, and my brother's invitation—an epiphany hit me.

My physical body, every ability I have, and my passions and talents are supposed to bring God glory. I'd always asked God to get on board with my great plans—to be an NFL champion, to have the microphone in my face, to be part of a Super Bowl win. But I wasn't sure that I'd ever worked for all that to bring glory to God. I knew it was time to ask myself tough questions and be bold enough to answer honestly.

Had I been doing all this (chasing football) for God or for me? When I answered truthfully, I realized it had been for me. I love football; I love the game and the competition and the comradery, but I was doing it for *my* benefit, *my* glory. I realized Arena football was not part of any plan I'd ever had. And in that same moment, I realized I wanted to make a bigger difference than what playing in the league another two to ten years could offer. I didn't want to end up with nothing, to live a life without significance, to have nothing to show for God's gifts but a broken body, and I certainly didn't want to end up wondering who I was without the sport of football.

> *Do not be deceived: God is not mocked, for whatever one sows, that will he also reap. For the one who sows to his own flesh will from the flesh reap corruption, but the one who sows to the Spirit will from the Spirit reap eternal life. And let us not grow weary of doing good, for in due season we will reap, if we do not give up* (Galatians 6:7–10).

God's wisdom poured through me in this season of my life. I discovered that it's not just about doing what we consider good deeds for the sake of doing good deeds. Even if we do "good deeds," if we do them with the wrong heart position, are they still good?

God knows the difference between a heart bent toward worldly success and one bent toward glorifying Him. If what we're sowing is motivated by a selfish, sinful, even deceived heart, then what we reap won't be good; it won't glorify God. Even though it may look good on the outside (chasing an NFL dream while giving thanks to God), that doesn't mean it is good.

The most important part of our choices and actions is not the choice or action itself, or even the result of the action. What's most important is our heart's position throughout the process. If we sow (work) from a heart that is submitted to Christ and want His will above all else, we will reap God's goodness and feel fulfilled as we live out His will for us.

All of my thoughts had now turned toward the scourge of drug abuse in our country. My deepest desire became to get the word out about the dangers and grief that come with drug use. So I asked the only question I knew to ask at that point: *God, what do you want me to do?*

I spoke with my parents, and we prayed together. My plan was to go to LA, live with Conard, work in modeling and acting to make ends meet, and write a script about my brother's life and the reality of how drugs destroy lives and devastate families. My goal was to ensure no one ever had to experience what we did—that people would stop turning to drugs at all.

Hope was building inside me as I planned my future. I felt peace about my decision to lay down my football career. I just had to decide when. My parents were somewhat surprised and wanted me to be sure of the decision. I knew I was sure.

The Arena football season wasn't over yet, and I was just healthy enough where I could practice, and I did. For two weeks, I was back on the field—not back on the active roster but at least playing again. And it was going well. While not one hundred percent, I was adjusting to the activity, needling my body back into football condition. But my heart wasn't in the same place.

Sam knew about my pending decision. I'd been on the injured reserve list for seven or eight weeks. There were four weeks left in the season and the team was hoping for a playoff berth when I confided in him it was time for me to retire. My perspective was this: If I knew this wasn't what my life was about anymore, it made sense to call it. Why even finish out the season? Looking back, I could have finished the season and honored my commitment to the team, but I figured if football wasn't my mission, my God-anointed path, why prolong it? If I wasn't doing life for me anymore but for God, why do football for another day?

After practice on that final Monday, I asked Sam to throw the ball with me one more time. At that moment, he knew it was the end. We would play these games where he'd throw a set number of passes (like ten), running me in different patterns that he'd call, and I had to catch them all to finish and head to the locker room. This time, he didn't make the game very easy.

About halfway through the set, I got emotional. *This is it,* I thought. *I'm about to take off my pads for the last time.* This dream and the journey to reach it, all that I had worked for my entire life, were coming to a close. I took solace in the knowledge I was giving it all to God, but I still felt the sadness and the loss, rushing through me.

I started to cry. That caused me to drop a couple of Sam's passes. The waterworks behind the facemask had prevented me from seeing the ball clearly. According to our unofficial game rules, we had to start the process again. "Oh, my gosh! How long are we going to be out here?" he said with a knowing smile. He still didn't make the next ten passes easy.

Once the game was over, Sam gave me a fist bump, and we hugged. I left for the locker rooms, took off my pads, showered, and grabbed my playbook. Then I went to Coach Hohensee's door and knocked.

"Coach Hohensee, I just want to thank you for the opportunity to play pro football and for believing in me. You and the rest of the coaching staff and organization have treated me wonderfully the whole time I've been here. Thanks for giving me time with my family after my brother passed and for giving me the chance to rehab after my injury. My brother's death has really caused me to reevaluate what's important in life. I love the game of football, but I feel led to go down another path. Thank you again for everything, Coach!"

Coach Hohensee looked at me, feeling dumbfounded. He couldn't believe what I was saying. But he wished me the best of luck. I laid my playbook on his desk and walked out of his office. I had officially retired from pro football.

A few minutes later, I loped back to the apartment building, packed up my Jeep Cherokee, turned in my apartment keys, and headed west.

RED ZONE CHECK

1. Are you surprised by my decision to suddenly retire from football? I'm sure you're heard stories of others giving up dreams or certain comforts to follow God's call on their lives, to make a greater impact on this world. The best examples were Jesus's disciples. What do you make of those who do this? Have you ever felt God lead you to give up or lay down something you love for a different calling? How did you respond? (Luke 9:33, Luke 14:33)

2. If we don't like what we are reaping, we can change what we are sowing. What have you been reaping lately? Self-glory or selflessness? What has been sown as a result? Are there things you can change today to set yourself up for a better harvest? (2 Corinthians 9:10)

Chapter 14

THE SEARCH

I want to tell tales of love and that includes God's grace, mercy, love, honor, and faithfulness. But I am still in my own way.
My Journal Entry, October 11, 2004

Los Angeles, specifically Hollywood, was a different world from where I had come and even from what I was used to in the sports world. The entertainment and modeling industry gauges success and worth against the standards of wealth, fame, and beauty. People are evaluated and celebrated against these superficial measures, which was hard because for my whole life, success and worth had come from hard work and achievement. In my old world, not the nicest car, but one's character mattered. A formula existed that had made sense to me. You work on strength, you'll get stronger. You work on speed, you'll get faster. You watch more film, your understanding will improve. So it might come as no surprise that my time in California produced a lot of opportunities *and insights*—some good, some surprising, and some not so great.

When my Jeep Cherokee first landed at my brother Conard's place in late spring 2004, I had every intention of writing the screenplay of Jacob's life and getting it made into a film or docuseries. I wanted to use his story to help release the stronghold addiction had over others and glorify God. I believed this was the Lord's new purpose for my life.

I found a talent agent, secured a manager, and began the work of making connections in a place where connections are the only things that propel you forward. I attended castings for acting jobs and commercials, and a few of those experiences brought some exciting opportunities.

I auditioned for the role of Superman in a movie, for the TV show *Smallville*, and for one of the X-Men movies. I was met with moderate success and made the money that would have allowed me to earn a good living.

One especially exciting opportunity came when I ended up in the movie, *We are Marshall*, the story of the Marshall University football squad and coaches who died in the plane crash in 1970. This story was meaningful to my family, dear to our hearts, because my dad almost attended Marshall after being recruited to play football. He ultimately chose West Virginia University, but many of his friends, the guys he played with or competed against in high school (in Huntington, West Virginia where Marshall is located), or those he worked out with in the off-seasons, died in that crash. Even my dad's childhood doctor was on that plane.

When I heard about the movie, I thought *I have to figure out a way to be in this thing.* After phoning my manager and explaining the significance, I ended up securing a role as a "special ability extra," doing football stunts. The producers and crew shot the movie over a three-month period, including the iconic and moving speech Coach Jack Lengyel—played by Matthew McConaughey—made at the graveyard in Huntington. I stayed with my sister, Sheryl, who lived across the river in Proctorville, Ohio, while filming that scene. If you pause the movie at just the right moment, you can see my face as the camera pans across the players during the coach's motivating speech.

Through all of this, I didn't forget about Jacob's story, but I'd never written a screenplay before. Writing out a story and writing a screenplay are not the same types of writing. There's an art to drafting screenplays. I didn't want my first attempt to be the one about Jacob's life because I didn't know what I was doing. I couldn't afford to mess this up. I wanted this movie to be excellent, to give it my very best.

By the grace of God, I met a young actor named Chris Ackerman—a true brother in Christ—who would later become one of my best friends. Chris starred in the movie *Elektra* with the well-known actress Jennifer Garner. Our friendship grew into a writing partnership as we worked on developing a script together for a story we created from our imaginations. We put in many hours at local coffee shops to write and edit for several months. In the end, it didn't end up getting picked up or going anywhere. But we gained valuable experience, and eventually, we wrote and co-directed a short film together for a Christian film festival called the 168, so named for the 168 hours in which your film must be written, shot, and edited.

As the months went by, I felt repulsed by the worldliness and seediness within LA. It's a cesspool of perversity, and many times, I found myself sickened by what I saw and what I had to throw my hand up and say no to. The decision-makers can make things happen for people, but often they want things in return—things I wasn't willing to do. Though it wasn't always an easy choice. My agent and I had long discussions about which roles I would even screen-test or audition for, based on my values. I wrestled with what, if any, concessions I needed to make to succeed. Of course, there was a part of me that wanted people to recognize me—to find stardom and be labeled "attractive," especially after being ridiculed in high school, called "Jerry," and more. I had to intentionally draw lines and hold those lines despite a lot of push-back from a lot of directions and the offer of money. I constantly had to ask myself, "Who am I?" and "What do I believe in?" I struggled with boundaries, sometimes not knowing what I was getting into until I was at the audition or photoshoot or on location. The pressure to take the bait that dangled in front of me was intense.

During this season of testing, I drew strength from my experiences, especially my time at Yale. It may surprise you to find out that Yale University was originally founded in 1701 by congregationalist ministers to fight growing liberalism at Harvard. Today, Yale has strayed radically from its humble Christian roots to the point of being a bastion for liberal thought and secularism. I took the course called New Testament Literature and History my first semester as a freshman, excited for all I would learn because it was actually being taught by the head of the religious studies department. I assumed, maybe naively, that the professor would be a Christian. To my shock and dismay, he was not a believer, and he taught the class from a completely secular point of view. He repeatedly called out believers in class, including me, for our faith and asked us to defend our beliefs. This pattern didn't just happen in the classroom, it happened all over campus. I was cornered at the lunch table by intelligent students convinced they could rely on their own minds and strength. I had to make a choice: did I really believe the things I professed, or was I just a product of my upbringing? I studied the Word with more fervor and made religious philosophy, specifically Christian Apologetics, my minor. I started taking classes at the divinity school and armed myself to give a reason for the hope that I have in Christ.

This experience, like all the testing we face, is for our good because it refines and strengthens us. By the grace of God, I didn't have to face this time alone. I had my teammates in our football Bible study and John Hardie, as well as other AIA attenders. That community helped encourage me, yet we were definitely in the minority on campus. Similarly, my Hollywood experience tested my beliefs and my resolve. Temptations were placed in front of me with the implied promise that if I succumbed, I could have everything I've ever wanted.

This is how Satan operates. He's a liar and a thief. He wants to deceive you, entrap you and ultimately use your sin to destroy you. At every step in my journey, Jesus never left my side, and God has also always provided someone, at least one brother or sister in Christ, to stand with me. LA was no different. Though we were surrounded by worldliness and extreme darkness, God connected me with other brothers to go to war with.

> *Though one may be overpowered, two can defend themselves. A cord of three strands is not quickly broken* (Ecclesiastes 4:12).

I already mentioned Chris Ackerman. We originally met at a bar called CLEAR where Conard was the VIP security manager. The modeling and acting gigs were inconsistent, so I needed a reliable income; however, I also needed flexibility to go on the casting calls. As we became closer friends, I even invited Chris to a Billy Graham crusade, where Chris responded to an altar call, completely giving his heart to Jesus. Besides Chris Ackerman, I met Josh Holt and Josh Reeves, who would grow to become some of my best friends in the world.

While these opportunities and my new friends were a gift, I didn't love acting and modeling overall. I didn't love the way Hollywood valued the superficial things of this world, and even more so, I didn't respect what others were doing to get ahead in the industry. The world is like that, and it didn't necessarily surprise me, but it was hard to be in that environment all of the time. I asked God what to do . . . I asked Him to show me what He was doing. Because I just didn't know.

As usual, God was working all things for good, for His glory.

As a former pro athlete, I was used to working out five or six hours per day, training for my sport. Since the modeling and acting jobs were inconsistent, I couldn't have a normal life. There were many days where I had nothing to do except work out, play basketball with friends, and write. Deciding to apply my work ethic to my new life, I took acting classes at the best studios and spent hours practicing this new craft.

One casting agent told my talent agent that I had a lisp and recommended I work on getting rid of it. Interestingly, I don't have a lisp (and never did), but I was prepared to do anything and everything the casting agents told me to do, so I hired a voice coach. I quickly realized they specialize in accents, not speech issues, so that didn't work. While trying to find speech therapy services I could afford, I stumbled across "student therapy." When clinicians are still in graduate school, they are allowed to treat patients under the supervision of a licensed therapist. It's the way students log hours toward graduation requirements. For patients, it's a less expensive alternative to get their therapy.

On my first day, as I sat in the waiting room, a beautiful girl, one of the therapists, walked out to call the patient seated next to me back for therapy. During my hour-long session, where I was forced to repeat the *S* sound by reading phrases from a deck of cards made for children that my therapist showed me—*Sally sells seashells by the seashore*—I built up the nerve to ask her about the other therapist.

"Oh, it's Kelly. Do you know her?" my therapist asked.

"I'd like to know her."

"She's a sweet girl . . ."

"Well, I'm a nice guy!"

My speech therapist never introduced me to Kelly, but she must have said something to her because the next time I sat in the waiting room and Kelly walked through, she wouldn't even look at me. Well, that drove me all the more. It had become a *game of pursuit.*

After a few weeks of therapy, I was discharged. I found Kelly at the water fountain in the back of the clinic, and for ten minutes, we talked and discovered we attended the same church, Bel Aire Presbyterian Church. I asked her if she wanted to connect at the next young adult/college meet up. We did, and afterward, we went to Starbucks together. *The rest is history*, as they say.

Three years later, at our rehearsal dinner, I learned that my speech therapist had recorded our sessions when the audio from the day I had asked about Kelly played over the sound system at the restaurant. Everyone had a good laugh—me included.

Within a year and a half of living in California, my mission perspective changed. Feeling fed up with not having any sense of fulfillment in the acting and modeling business, working in an industry that was as seedy and unscrupulous as it was, and being away from football long enough to realize I wouldn't stop missing it, fueled the change. My heart was breaking with what was happening in the world of acting and modeling, and my soul needed some distance from it.

When I quit pro ball, the pain of letting it go made it hard to watch football on TV or take part in the fantasy football craze, which had become popular by this time. This sport that I loved, that I had walked away from, I missed. It felt like something significant had been ripped from my life. And I wondered what God was up to as my longing to play and be around the game continued to eat away at me.

I got involved with football again. I missed the way I had always gotten results for the effort I had put in. Regardless if you win or not, hard work always pays off in the athletic world. It stands in stark contrast to the entertainment industry, which is all about who you know and what lengths you'll stoop to be successful. I did not want to get involved with that. None of it sat well with me.

God loves when we choose to trust Him; it brings Him glory, and He delights in our confidence in Him. God made *faith* a key to unlocking His greatest blessings. Often, to get where God wants us to go, we have to take blind steps, move forward (like to California), even though we can barely see a few inches in front of our faces. God had given me enough prompting to move in a new direction, and He wanted me to take those steps *in faith*, to trust that He would put my feet on solid ground. When I did, His goodness was evident.

> *And without faith it is impossible to please God, because anyone who comes to him must believe that he exists and that he rewards those who earnestly seek him* (Hebrews 11:6).

I had spent so much time in my life trying to prepare to be the best football player I could be, with God's nudging, I thought, *Maybe I can give back and help others do that.* That's when I started coaching at Santa Monica High School. It gave me the sense of living in the world of sports again while offering me mini opportunities to step out of the disreputable entertainment industry, if only for short stints.

That first season, in 2006, the Santa Monica High School football team had a pretty good year, even competing for the conference championship. The experience solidified things for me—in my head and in my heart, and I caught "the coaching bug." My "Hollywood mission" wasn't what I thought it would be, and coaching not only made good use of my talents, experiences, and passion, it was *fun.*

I started making calls. As you've learned by now, I'm a goal-oriented person, and whenever I set my sights on something, I work hard to get it. Coaching at the college level was my next goal. Some of the calls I made were to my former Yale coaches. They pointed me to Wagner

College, a Division I AA school on Staten Island in New York, which was looking for a defensive backs coach. They even recommended me to the school. Wagner interviewed me over the phone, and shortly afterward, offered me the job.

But I had this girlfriend now—Kelly—and we had reached the point in our relationship where it was going really well. We talked about the job offer and wondered if we should continue to date while I left for New York and she stayed in Los Angeles. I made it clear in our discussions that continuing our relationship was my intention. I wanted to keep what we had already built, if not continue to see where it would lead. Kelly agreed. For both of us, in some ways, the distance solidified our relationship. People say absence makes the heart grow fonder. For the next year, it was true for us.

Hired as a position coach and also a GA—a grad assistant coach—I had to take classes to meet the requirements of the job. Despite what other GAs thought, I considered this an awesome opportunity to earn my MBA (Master of Business Administration). At almost twenty-seven years old, I knew it would add to my professional development and possibly open more career doors down the road. Again, true to my nature, I finished my MBA in just eighteen months, working while taking a full load of classes each semester and through the summer.

As a defensive backs coach, I had good success that first year. I had trained under some fantastic coaches in the past, and I used that experience. In my second year at Wagner, the head coach, Walt Hameline, promoted me, and I added "co-special teams coordinator" to my resume. This was an amazing opportunity because I was tasked with recruiting players from Florida and California, two places I knew well and that generally produced a tremendous amount of talent.

Everything in sports is competitive, including the coaching gigs. The goal is to bring in the most (and best) recruits. That first year of recruiting, I hit the road running in November (later than most) and ended up bringing a lot of talented tape back. My strength was loving on the kids. As with most things in life, relationship-building mattered. That season, I secured the second highest number of recruits. The challenge fueled me, and the next year, I had the most recruits with thirteen. And the team did well. In the 2007 and 2008 seasons, Wagner had the number-one-ranked total defense in the NEC (Northeast Conference). We didn't end up winning the championship, but we were close.

That second year at Wagner also gave me the chance to have an unexpected reunion. Coach Hameline was looking for a wide receivers' coach to join the staff. My old buddy, Ivery Gaskin, was in the middle of a significant life transition and wasn't happy at his current job. IG had never finished his degree at UCF; he was only a few credits short. He had left to go to Canada to play football in an attempt to earn money for his growing family. I knew the type of work ethic and leadership he would bring to the table. But it's pretty unconventional to hire a coach for a graduate assistant position when they have yet to finish their undergraduate degree. Coach Hameline took a chance on Ivery, and we got to be roommates as well. It helped make the gloomy Northeastern days and all the hours we put in a lot more enjoyable.

Ivery has since revealed to me how impactful that time was on his life. Not having a college degree was a limiting factor for him in terms of moving up the corporate ladder, and it capped his pay. After graduating from Wagner, that degree has exponentially increased his earnings, becoming a real blessing for him and his family.

But he had started all this by blessing me years earlier. See, when I felt unwanted, left-out, and passed over by that UF wide receiver years before at FAST, Ivery had heard my conversation with the trainers while running on the treadmill. He later told me he felt moved to approach me, to "right the wrong." I think, first, because he saw someone hurting but, second, he didn't want me to perceive African Americans in a negative light. Our friendship is not based on color; it transcends it. But how would either of us have known at the time what his small act of kindness would lead to? So I encourage you. When you see someone hurting or in need, don't dismiss that urge you feel in your gut to do something. It might make an eternal impact on their life, and only God knows how He will use it in yours.

Life was going well. I had my MBA and a successful coaching career. I had a steady girlfriend, and life felt good. During my time at Wagner, while she was still living in California, I asked Kelly to marry me.

RED ZONE CHECK

1. God moved Abraham out of Ur. God moved the Israelites through the desert and eventually to the promised land. And God moved me to California. Just because God moves us somewhere new, it doesn't mean it's an easy road to travel. And it doesn't mean it's permanent. We still need faith to get us through. Has God moved you somewhere you weren't expecting to go? Was the journey smooth from the start, or did you face obstacles, struggle, or perhaps disappointment? What did God do with that? (Genesis 12:1)

2. Has your faith ever been attacked? Have you been called out to defend what you believe, to prove that the Bible is true, or accused of being" anti-science" because of your faith? How did you respond? Were you able to effectively articulate why you believe in Jesus? If not, what will you do moving forward to arm yourself for these interactions? (1 Peter 3:15)

3. My success at Wagner, in part, was because of my ability to build relationships with people, specifically the kids I was recruiting and then coaching. Where in your life can you build relationships and show the love of Christ to those around you? (1 Corinthians 9:22)

Chapter 15

THE MOUNTAIN

The search for love is one of the hardest
and deepest challenges I will face.
My Journal Entry, December 17, 2005

Kelly said yes.

We knew we wanted to take part in premarital counseling. There are many reasons for this: A counselor will not only enlighten couples with their insight, but will also teach them some strategies to help them make their marriage the best it can be. They offer neutral opinions about compatibility and address possible pitfalls. Kelly and I enlisted my dad's best friend, Don Meredith, and his wife, Sally—the founders of Christian Family Life and co-authors of the book *Two Becoming One*. The time spent with this wise couple was incredible, and we received an enormous amount of knowledge and feedback.

During the last session, Sally spoke privately with Kelly, and I met with Don. I don't know what Sally told Kelly, but the information Don gave me was unforgettable. In part, he requested I take some time to pray.

"Josh, Kelly is an amazing girl. She has the foundation and innate qualities to be an incredible spouse, including some strong character traits. She is a sweet and tender-hearted girl, and we can see why you love her.

"But, Josh, we worry because she seems to carry some significant insecurities, which I believe will affect your relationship. I'm afraid they may compromise the way you're able to live your life and do what you're designed to do."

"What do you mean?" I asked.

"Because she doesn't like attention, for herself or for you, you two might struggle. You're an outgoing and gregarious guy, and your achievement-oriented philosophy and goals and your level of self-motivation are off the charts. I don't know if she's going to come alongside you in your professional endeavors, and it may affect how you're able to interact with people as you move through your career."

My heart flapped against my rib cage. I could see his perspective, but I also believed our relationship's strengths and our commitment to communication were strong enough to overcome anything. Plus, I loved Kelly.

Don continued, "Josh, you need to ask God if this is a mountain He's asking you to climb . . . because you may have to climb it for the rest of your life. You may never get to the top. You can't love someone enough to love them out of the way they feel about themselves. So I encourage you to pray about it. Ask the Lord: Is this a battle He wants you to fight? Whatever decision you make, we'll support you guys. If you choose to move forward in marriage, we'll be standing behind you and encouraging you both."

I left the session feeling overwhelmed. Marriage, a lifelong commitment, is not something to take lightly. I sought God and asked for His direction, but I never felt like I received a clear answer. So my final prayer became a summary of my newfound knowledge, my assumptions, my understanding of God's character, and my choice: *God, you made me strong. I can handle adversity. And maybe You made me strong for this very reason. Kelly and I, with You at our sides, will fight through these issues, and we'll overcome them . . . In Jesus's name. Amen.*

No matter who is involved, every marriage unites two broken people who come into a covenant with wounds, flaws, and sin. Every individual believes their family of origin and the experiences they had in that family are normal. When we marry someone, we're trying to build a new normal. And I believe there is little hope for an exceptional marriage unless Christ is the center.

I'm not saying there aren't marriages that succeed apart from Jesus. However, I believe those marriages often turn into something akin to formal arrangements, ones based on performance and lofty expectations. Marriages without the love of Christ at the center—as with any other relationship—usually carry what I call the *responsibility of happiness* promise. The union becomes a transactional relationship. You'll hear it in the form of spouses who say, "I'm going to make you happy." What they mean is, "If you make me happy (perform), I'll make you happy (reciprocate)." Or, at best, "Let's make each other happy." Over time, this evolves into a marriage comprising two roommates, filled with performance fatigue, who find they're both *un*happy. The happiness promise and the performance it requires to maintain are not God-approved responsibilities for spouses to carry. Our responsibility is to love each other as God loves us. The only way we can establish a lasting, godly marriage is to place Jesus at the center and allow ourselves to be transformed by the work of the Holy Spirit inside ourselves, as we mutually sacrifice for one another. Most importantly, we have to abide in Christ, to take our very nutrients for life from Him. We cannot take our identity or value from our mate; it has to come from God alone.

> *Whoever confesses that Jesus is the Son of God, God abides in him, and he in God. So we have come to know and to believe the love that God has for us. God is love, and whoever abides in love abides in God, and God abides in him (1 John 4:15–16).*

So I pressed forward, and Kelly and I married on November 28, 2008. It was a beautiful wedding, a dream come true, filled with family and friends.

As the weeks and months went by, it grew more apparent that our relationship was not perfect, and I was reminded of the premarital counseling in which we had participated. The fundamental problem in the beginning was that our conflict management styles differed, and that created issues almost immediately. I leaned toward talking things out, pursuing more communication and discussion, even if that meant engaging in conflict. Kelly leaned toward avoiding conflict altogether, which often led to a lack of communication and shutting down in self-protection. Most marriages unite one of each kind of person. But there was more . . .

Kelly had grown up in a Christian home. Her family were regular church attenders. And when we met in California, she was going to the young adult group at the same church as me. I knew she had a relationship with God, but we had never prayed together. Even after our wedding, Kelly chose not to pray out loud with me, and I believe intimacy grows between two people when they engage in the spiritual connection produced by praying together. There is a vulnerability to baring our hearts in prayer and often, as we open our lips to pray, God molds and shapes our hearts.

People think intimacy is always about sex. But intimacy is about truth. When you realize you can tell someone anything, when you can show your whole self to them, when you can stand in front of them and be vulnerable—whatever that looks like for you—and their response is, "You're safe with me," that's intimacy.

Instead of connecting with God alongside Kelly and growing in intimacy, I asked her for prayer requests, and then I'd pray for her.

As usually happens, the lack of spiritual intimacy led to decreased intimacy in other areas of our relationship as well, including emotional intimacy, physical intimacy, and trust. It was proving to be a tall mountain to climb.

After our wedding came the end of my second year at Wagner college, and I graduated with my MBA. Because I had graduated, I could no longer be a GA, so I set my sights on the next level.

Pat Graham, a former teammate from Yale, was coaching at Notre Dame under Charlie Weis. Pat put in a good word for me with Charlie, and I found myself in conversations with the Fighting Irish about coming on staff. Pat also had connections with the New England Patriots because of Coach Weis and put me in contact with them, hoping to help me land a job. The Patriots had already won three super bowl championships by that time. I couldn't believe it; I was having conversations with both Notre Dame and New England. I was never officially offered a job by Bill Belichick and the Patriots, but it didn't matter. I wasn't going to work for either program . . .

Kelly, who had told Don and Sally Meredith that she supported my career and everything that came along with it—who'd said she understood the transient nature of coaching and agreed to move if needed—seemed to have changed her mind. "I won't go," she told me. "I'm not going to move away from California."

This was a blow to me and our marriage. I knew I couldn't ascend any type of coaching career ladder without the ability to follow the open opportunities. Frustration embedded its tentacles into my gut where it would continue to fester. And I lost some of the trust I had for Kelly. *Had she just agreed to whatever she thought I wanted to hear before we were married? What else hasn't she told me?* The questions swirled in my head.

Despite our relationship struggles and feeling boxed into a location on the map, I loved my wife and wanted to be with her. However, I also did everything I could to find a compromise that would suit us both. My parents had worked for Joe Gibbs Racing for twenty years by this point. I contacted the race team and worked out a deal (since I had my MBA) to come aboard in a marketing position—one that would put me on the pit crew for one of their lower level teams. I could work my way up to the NASCAR pit crew if my times for changing tires were good enough. I'd still be an athlete, so this was a great option for me, one that would be more stable than coaching. The job was in Charlotte, North Carolina. It wasn't the cold northeast, in Foxborough, Massachusetts, where the Patriots play, or the windy Midwest, in South Bend, Illinois, where Notre Dame is located. Don and Sally Meredith lived in Charlotte, so Kelly and I had been there and knew people who lived there. It's a beautiful city with temperatures more closely aligned with California's. So I brought the idea to Kelly.

In short, she said no.

Kelly made it clear: she would not move. She had grown up in a family that had built long-standing roots in their California community. Her mom and sister both taught at the elementary school where Kelly and her sister had played on the playground as kids. Moving out of state to follow someone's career had been a normal part of my family's journey, but not hers. And she dug in her heels.

I felt blindsided. Her refusal to compromise—and unwillingness to move and support my career aspirations—left me deflated. If I wanted my marriage to survive, I was going to have to choose to stay in California, effectively forcing me out of a dream job . . . perhaps out of my career. I could try to find a coaching job at USC or UCLA, but in this industry, it's hard to break into schools where you don't have any connections. It's very much a "who you know" type of industry. Owners, college presidents, athletic directors, and head coaches need to trust the people they hire. I potentially had that type of "in"—that opportunity to move into the pipeline—at Notre Dame under Charlie Weis, through Pat Graham. But my choice to marry Kelly and make our relationship my priority had blocked me from saying yes to that pipeline.

The saying is true: Opposites tend to be attracted to each other. A quiet individual might gravitate toward a significant other who is talkative. A fast-paced city girl might fall in love with a laid-back country boy. Unfortunately, as relationships progress, opposites also *attack*. For every strength or character trait we initially fall in love with, there is another side of that coin, one where that strength, when taken too far, morphs into a weakness, or at least something that rubs our spouses the wrong way. And if that alternate side of the coin is not dealt with, it can produce a lot of conflict. I am notably a go-getter and quite extroverted. Kelly is the opposite—content and reserved.

However, what really makes a marriage relationship so difficult to maintain is that we, as a product of our sinful nature, are wired to think about ourselves first. I don't mean we're all narcissists, but our reflex reaction, given any choice, is to look out for ourselves. Jesus's brother mentioned something about this:

> *What is the source of wars and fights among you? Don't they come from your passions that wage war within you?* (James 4:1).

These passions and waging wars are the longings of our sinful, selfish hearts. We want what's best for us. And many of us hope, even if unconsciously or subconsciously, that our spouses will let us get our way. Striving to fulfill our desires and needs leads to conflict. Conflict, when not handled well, causes that gut-twisting frustration I experienced with Kelly. When we're part of a marriage experiencing these kinds of struggles, we wonder what's wrong.

Every marriage is hard because the transition from living as two individuals to living as one (the phenomena of two becoming one as described in Genesis) isn't a natural process. It's a divinely inspired one. And it takes a God-centered focus to achieve and live out well.

> *And above all these put on love, which binds everything together in perfect harmony. And let the peace of Christ rule in your hearts, to which indeed you were called in one body. And be thankful* (Colossians 3:14–15).

This love of Christ, which doesn't come from our flesh, is what binds us together and creates harmony. It is a love born from the gravity of our savior's costly sacrifice for us. Jesus' death is to our gain, it gives us life, but it also humbles us. When that love rules our hearts, we can be truly selfless.

In January 2009, I moved back to California to be with my wife, though I had no job. It was not the start to married life I had dreamed about, but I loved Kelly, and I had made a promise to her when I had recited my vows. Aside from my relationship with Christ, she was my priority. I was determined to *climb the mountain*, as Don Meredith warned we might need to do. After all, it was no longer all about me. Two had become one.

RED ZONE CHECK

1. Has anyone ever changed their mind or not held true to something they had assured you of—a value, a faith, a promise, a perspective, or a standard? How did it make you feel when they changed their mind? Could you understand their point of view? Did you try? Was there an opportunity to compromise? If not, what happened? Did this cause you to question God's honesty, His faithfulness? If hurt from a past relational disappointment still lingers, are you willing to repent of holding onto that bitterness, not just with the person but with God? (Colossians 3:13)

2. Our relationship with our spouse is meant to mimic the unity of Christ and the Church. Do you have good role models in your life that portray this type of marriage? One where the love of Christ is at the center and the two individuals have set aside themselves to be united as one, under God's direction, provision, and grace? If you don't have good role models for what marriage should look like, where might you find those role models? (Ephesians 5:22–33)

Chapter 16

THE GOLDEN STATE

God has already bestowed manhood on you,
and you are very much a warrior.
My Journal Entry, November 22, 2005

I hoped sunny California would bring back the warmth in Kelly's and my relationship as I moved into her apartment in Sherman Oaks.

She left for work every day, but without a job, I couldn't do the same. I knew I loved coaching, so I spent hours looking for a school nearby that needed a football coach. Eventually, I was offered an amazing opportunity on the coaching staff at the University of Hawaii, with the help of my former NFL Europe defensive backs coach, Jeff Reinebold. Kelly said she'd be willing to check it out, so we flew out there, and while there, I was officially offered the job. Almost immediately after we returned, I received a call. "Josh, I'm sorry, but Coach June Jones's buddy was fired at another school and needs a place to land, so he's going to give him the job." Another closed door.

Later that same year, 2009, I was hired by Los Angeles Pierce Junior College as the defensive coordinator for their football team. The previous season, the team had gone 2–8, and they had not won a conference championship in nearly twenty years. Junior college coaching stipends are not really enough to make a living on unless you can secure a teaching job as well.

Luckily, with my MBA that I just earned at Wagner, I could get hired to teach in the Business Department. The students in my introductory level business class were a mix of people, hailing from different communities and generations, and all with different motives and goals. Some students were fresh out of high school; others were adults in their forties and fifties who already had real-world business experience. I thrived with the challenge the diversity afforded.

While Pierce's football team had not experienced a winning season in a long time, these years would be some of the most impactful years of coaching I would ever enjoy. These young men came from the greater LA region, including the inner city—not an easy place to grow up. There was both a Crip and a Blood gang member on the team. On the field, they practiced hard. Off the field, these guys had guns stashed in their cars and wanted to kill each other.

The other members of the team were talented kids who weren't eligible to play in college because of lackluster grades or who were somehow missed or didn't get recruited for a myriad of reasons. Maybe they were too small or not strong enough yet. Others were moderately skilled high school players who wanted to keep playing the game. Many of the players didn't have fathers in their lives, and I had the privilege of being a male influence. I took that role seriously.

A quote from Proactive Coaching caught my attention one day, and it's lived inside me ever since: "One of the most important kids you will ever coach is the one who needs the program more than the program needs (them)." I wanted to be a part of a program that realized that truth and catered to those kids, and at Pierce, I found that program.

Not long after getting hired, I started an FCA (Fellowship of Christian Athletes) huddle at Pierce, and soon, roughly thirty-five players were showing up to the meetings. Something in my heart broke for these kids, and I realized, yet again, that God uses everything. My missed opportunities to coach Division I football had culminated in this experience, where God was orchestrating a Kingdom impact in the lives of these young men—through me.

The first season I was there, the Pierce football team turned their *W*s and *L*s around, going 7–3 and winning the conference championship. I loved every minute of what I was doing. And it wasn't just because the team now had a winning season. It was so much more than that.

One night, while flipping channels, I caught an expose on ESPN about P3, Peak Performance Project, based in Santa Barbara. Dr. Marcus Elliott, a Harvard-trained medical doctor, had started the program to train elite athletes. My mind went back in time to my experience with the Chris Carter FAST Program.

Dr. Elliott had worked with the Patriots and was well known in the sports industry for reducing hamstring injuries in athletes. He'd even been consulted by the NFL to help with injury reduction. P3 looked amazing, so I reached out and set up a meeting with Dr. Elliott. During our sit-down, I quickly realized I was sitting across from one of the sharpest guys I'd ever met.

"I want to work with athletes and help them become the best versions of themselves, help them max out their potential. I'm a gifted athlete, but I was never the most athletic guy on any of the teams I played. I was the underdog and learned how to out-work everyone else. I had to maximize everything I had to give myself the chance to compete at the highest level." I told Dr. Elliott about all of the re-starts I'd made through my career, training and retraining my body back into peak condition. I knew the process and knew it well.

"Josh, I love it. I think you can do this." Dr. Elliott offered me a paid internship with P3. He added, "But don't just be another 'ex-jock that simply trains athletes.' You're smart. So be a scientist." We came up with a plan for me to go back to school—this time at CSU, Northridge (a.k.a., California State University, Northridge or otherwise known as Cal State, Northridge) for their biomechanics and kinesiology program, which included motion analysis. I couldn't wait to get started.

During the late spring through the following summer months, while still coaching at Pierce, I worked at P3 in Santa Barbara, coached summer ball to help our guys get ready for the season, and took summer and fall classes at Cal State, Northridge.

One day, Dr. Elliott sat down with me. "Josh, I'm really close with the head strengthening coach at UC, Santa Barbara. His name is Dr. Jeremy Bettle." Later in Dr. Bettle's career, he would become the director of High Performance for the Brooklyn Nets, Toronto Maple Leafs, and Anaheim Ducks. I hadn't finished my master's degree yet, but Dr. Bettle hired me anyway. UCSB, a Division IA school, had every sport but football, so I worked with various athletes.

This new role filled my schedule. Once fall came, I woke up between 4:00 and 4:30 a.m. and drove the ninety minutes to Santa Barbara from Moorpark, California, where Kelly and I had moved. During those early morning commutes, I watched the sunrise while driving on the iconic 101—right along the coastline. Wow, is Santa Barbara beautiful! I'd coach the various sports teams at UCSB from 5:30 a.m. to noon, and then leave, driving straight to Cal State, Northridge, where I was enrolled in afternoon classes. Then, I'd hop back in the car and go to practice at Pierce, finally arriving home around 7:00 p.m. I traveled 130 miles every day in that season of my career, and I loved it. I cherished the ability to work with all of those athletes.

I continued to lead that FCA group at Pierce and kids' lives were changing every week. Those guys in the Crips and Bloods came together, finally playing as teammates on opposite sides of the field—the two corners that helped us win a championship. God was showing me how He was using me to make a difference in others' lives.

Soon, a kid from my past re-entered my life. There was a young man, Coleman Edmund, who had joined Wagner football as a true freshman the first year I arrived. He was a super talented kid—the fastest player on the team. He probably stood six foot two and weighed around 200 pounds. The head coach wanted to get something extra out of him because he was so athletic. Coach Hameline experimented with Coleman at wide receiver, QB, and returning kickoffs and punts—anything he could do to put the ball in his hands in space. But it just didn't seem to be a good fit, and Coleman continued to struggle. Coach came to me and explained that he was frustrated.

"He's too athletic not to be on the field. See if you can help him play defensive back."

Well, Coleman didn't want to tackle; he had an offensive mindset. He enjoyed the competitiveness of football, but the contact, not so much. He even joked about it, saying, "I'm trying to run away from getting hit. I'm not trying to hit anybody." And as a football coach, that's not the mentality you want your safety to have.

I was trying to ride Coleman to get something out of it, and of course, it wasn't working. At the end of the year, Coleman came to me and admitted he wanted to transfer to another school.

"How do I do this?"

"Well, I can't help you transfer, but I can look up some information to tell you how to get through the process. I was still trying to get him to stay."

Then, I lost touch with him. In January 2009, I found the job at Pierce. I don't know what laid it on my heart—though I know Who prompted me—but I found Coleman's number in my phone, and I reached out to see how he was doing.

"What's going on?"

"I'm at UCLA, running track." He had only been at UCLA for a semester. His plan was to be a walk-on for the football team that next summer and get a scholarship. I'm not sure how he was paying for the different paths he had taken. I hadn't had much interaction with his parents. But it sounded like he needed the financial help a scholarship could provide. He said he was bouncing around to stay with different people. He didn't talk about his family much, and it seemed he was trying to do a lot of this on his own.

"Coleman, if you want to play football, don't just walk on. If you love it there and want to stay there, then try it. But if your goal is to get a scholarship and you simply walk on, they own you. They don't have to give you a scholarship."

I knew he still had three full years of football eligibility left. "Coleman, come play junior college football for me at Pierce. You're going to have an incredible season and make a huge difference. We have college coaches that come here to recruit. You can get re-recruited. Just come for one semester, get your associate's degree, and then transfer anywhere."

Coleman said he needed a place to stay. I spoke with Kelly about it, and we invited him to live with us at our new home in Moorpark, California in 2009. He accepted.

Coleman was a great kid. We built a solid relationship, and it was different from what it had been at Wagner. God used this time. He stayed with us until the football season ended and earned the Player of the Year award. There were a couple of games in our 7–3 stretch that we wouldn't have won without Coleman. He was recruited by UC Berkeley, where he was given a scholarship. The coach who recruited Coleman to UC Berkeley had been the quarterback on the Amsterdam Admirals in the NFL Europe—Kevin Daft. This was one of the guys in that Bible study that convened in our hotel rooms in Amsterdam. Coleman was a perfect fit for his team, and that transfer put Kevin and me back in touch with each other.

Coleman played two more years before graduating with his bachelor's degree. I felt like I had impacted his life. We've stayed in touch, and Coleman now works in New York City and Houston, Texas, in the financial sector.

I believed this combination of jobs allowed me to fulfill my purpose. I wasn't a big-time collegiate football coach, but I trained and coached young athletes and be a part of watching them chase (and often reach) their dreams.

Soon after we reconnected, Kevin Daft approached me. "Hey, do you want to coach?"

As I thought about Kelly's adamant desire not to move away from California, I initially told him I wasn't sure. But Cal Berkeley was *in* California, within her boundary requirement, so I said, "If anything comes up, go ahead and drop my resume."

Well, along came a position—a strength and conditioning coaching role they called a *high performance specialist*. It was designed to support Cal Berkeley's initiative to take their program into the future, rebuilding, enhancing, and "earthquake-proofing" their entire athletic center and stadium. Mike Blasquez, the head strengthening coach, called me soon after Kevin dropped off my resume, while I was on a family vacation with Kelly and my parents.

My parents were thrilled, even jumping up and down as they congratulated me. I looked over at Kelly, and her mood was sullen. She went off by herself to cry because she didn't want to move, and that was heartbreaking for me. It was a moment I wanted to celebrate with her but couldn't.

The end of my time at Pierce felt heartbreaking, bittersweet. It was one of the hardest places to leave in all of my career. The little money I made there paled in comparison to the relationships I had built. When I told the kids I was leaving for a new role at Cal-Berkeley, they lined up, thirty-plus players strong, so they could each give me a hug and say goodbye. Snot from their tears collected on my shoulder as I moved down the line. Some of those tears were likely mine, as I was sobbing too. They knew, without a doubt, that I cared about them. And on that day, it was confirmed; they cared about me too.

My new commute to Cal Berkeley, as an assistant strength and conditioning coach, took me from warm and sunny Danville, California in the East Bay, west, through the tunnel toward San Francisco to Berkeley. During that drive, the temperature routinely dropped fifteen to twenty degrees, and the sun was stamped out by the mist and fog that rolled off of the waters of both the bay and the ocean. Driving home in the evenings, the beautiful weather from the valley would reappear, turning the sky brighter, which is what I preferred.

When I started at Cal Berkeley in August 2012, I thought I would be working directly for Mike Blasquez, the head strengthening and conditioning coach (soon to be the director of the high performance lab they were building). Instead, I fell under John Krasinski, an old-school strength and conditioning coach who was never involved in my hiring process. I liked John; he was a good strength coach with a great reputation in the field, but my instincts told me something was going on between him and the other coaches.

Cal was in the middle of their major overhaul when I first arrived—the construction of their multi-million dollar performance center, which included a new weight room, locker rooms, and coaches' offices. During the interim, the entire weight room, training room, and our offices were in a tent enclosure, which everyone called the SURGE, located on top of the hill at Berkeley.

I hit the ground at full speed in August since the team was heading into training camp, excited to use my experience at P3 and my education, having nearly finished my master's degree. Quickly, I realized why my resume had stood out to Head Coach Jeff Tedford. At the time, I was deep into research with Dr. Sean Flanagan, a young, published professor who was helping me with my thesis. We were assessing the effects of the position of the foot on jumping and whether dorsiflexion or plantarflexion mattered to the speed with which athletes could get off the ground and the height to which they could spring upward after jumping off of boxes.

Ultimately, we determined that intent (i.e., motivation) is what matters perhaps most, and I presented our research at the National Strength and Conditioning (NCSA) Conference, where I received the award for the best oral presentation of a thesis. Dr. Flanagan and I wrote up our findings, which were then published in the *Journal of Strength and Conditioning Research.*

Mike Blasquez had hired me to be part of this new high-performance initiative because I was a great fit, but John didn't seem interested in all the new technology, research, and findings. John was content to focus on the tried-and-true traditional strengthening exercises, including squats, bench presses, and clean lifts. When John didn't invite me to plan workouts or involve me with any strategy or decision-making sessions, I wondered if the thing I discerned to be "off" might be the head coach's plans to replace John . . . and maybe John knew that.

I'd ask John if I could have the workout cards to review, maybe even talk through them with him. I didn't get to see the new workout cards until the players saw them. I don't know if he thought I was an informant for Coach Tedford or Mike or what. Maybe he just wasn't interested in my input and was already certain of what he wanted to do and why. John was never rude to me; he simply had more of a command-and-control management style. "Josh, go watch those guys squat and take them through these warm-up exercises," he'd direct me. And that was it.

As the semester progressed, Coach Tedford asked me about the situation. "How are things going with John?" I assumed he was checking up, and it confirmed for me that something wasn't right between the levels above me. After that first season, at the end of 2012, John left the program.

Mike Blasquez quickly moved into the SURGE office with me until the new center was completed. Cal had the fourth-most football players of any college to advance to the NFL. Coach Tedford was doing an incredible job with recruiting and became the highest paid public employee in California. And for a short while, Cal-Berkeley rose as high as number two in the national polls, making all of our jobs exciting. I worked with all of the players but had the additional responsibility of working with the injured players, partnering with the head trainer, Wes McGaw, to write out their workouts and get them healthy as soon as possible. I followed Wes's guidelines regarding their restrictions and therapy goals and helped get them conditioned to play again. These players included future NFL stars and pro-bowlers, such as Keenan Allen (Chargers), Cameron Jordan (Saints), Michael Kendricks (fastest ever forty in the combine for an LB), Mitch Schwartz (Browns and later won a Super Bowl with the Chiefs), and CJ Anderson (Broncos).

Even though he was one of the sharpest guys I had met, Mike solicited my advice at every phase of the high-performance lab construction. I made recommendations regarding what equipment to purchase and where to place it. He put me in charge of the Polar program, which tracked the speed, heart rate, change in direction, and we even looked at cortisol levels to determine how our athletes were recovering. We sat together for long hours, sometimes working seventy hours per week, strategizing about seasonal workout plans to implement for winter break, spring break, and summer break. Some early mornings, I'd be at work by 5:00 or 6:00 in the morning. It was a complete one-eighty from when I reported to John.

I reveled in the work and the surrounding environment. One morning, an eight-point buck met me on the hill, and I feared it would charge at me, but by the grace of God, it didn't. I often watched our neighborhood mountain lion roam the hill across from SURGE.

My first year there, we missed the bowl game by one loss, to Washington. It was a disappointment, but the following season, we had a better record and went to the Holiday Bowl in San Diego to play the University of Texas Longhorns. We stayed at a beautiful hotel on the water, and someone from the Fellowship of Christian Athletes (FCA) got my name from someone who knew I was helping lead a Bible study for coaches—a group that included team chaplain, Kevin Knox, fellow strength coach, Chris DiSanto, running backs coach, Ron Gould, and even Kevin Daft at times. "Talk to Josh Phillips," they had told the FCA representative. FCA was hosting a prayer breakfast before the game. I got permission from Coach Tedford, and we brought about twenty players. Texas, coached by Mack Brown, brought their whole team.

We played a hard-fought game in which we lost. But being a part of it all made me feel important, valued, and . . . significant. I stared at my bowl ring, feeling the emotions of self-worth and pride, realizing they were things I had been chasing for years, and each opportunity, each job God had led me to, had paved a new stepping stone, creating a path that had led to that moment.

During the off-season, I ran strength and conditioning drills the football coaching staff couldn't specifically run per NCAA regulations. The benefit of my former experience as a defensive coach and having played pro ball catapulted me to a new level. When the new season arrived, I was asked to hold up the personnel cards for our defense on game day and wear a headset so I could hear the coaches' banter and decision-making as they and the owners spotted the game from their vantage points above. I was privy to coaching conversations and sat in on coaching meetings whenever I felt it would help. I flew on chartered jets; they fed me well, and I continued to work my tail off. Mike was an incredible boss and mentor.

Even though I was earning $45,000 per year, a third of what Mike was earning, I was working with a host of highly driven people, and each one inspired me. I didn't begrudge Mike's salary—or mine—but California is not an inexpensive place to live. So when Kelly and I started to talk about starting a family, my salary became a point of concern.

Kelly confided in me she hoped to leave her high-paying job as a licensed speech therapist to stay home with kids. I, too, wanted to be the provider for our family, but my current role would support none of these dreams. I resigned to the fact I'd have to look for other opportunities. It was a common practice for some coaches, when leaving for more advanced roles on other teams, to take assistants with them. I hoped someone might go to USC or another big-time football school, or even a nearby pro team, and invite me to go with them. Yet I had no control over what others did or what opportunities arose.

This new job hunt sent Kelly and me straight back to the initial issue we had faced in our fledgling marriage. At one point, a coach left for a new gig at Arizona, and he asked me about going with him. I knew Kelly wouldn't agree. I received job offers from Coastal Carolina and Bryant University in Rhode Island, but Kelly and I had reached a familiar and frustrating stalemate. She still wouldn't leave California. And we had never resolved the issue of how we each handled conflict. Even though she wanted to stay home with our future kids, and though I wanted to provide for my family, I felt my hands were tied to the Golden State once again. And the cuffs were tightening, wreaking havoc on any peace and understanding we had built up in our marriage.

Sam Clemons, one of my best friends and the quarterback from my days in Arena football—the same friend who drove me to the airport when my brother had passed away—moved back to California. He had built a thriving medical sales business and had been needling me for some time to come work for him. He knew me, knew my work ethic, and had been enticing me with promises of a much higher income for years. Finally, I reached the point where I felt so stuck between Kelly wanting me to get out of coaching, my desire to start a family, and not being able to create a job out of thin air that would pay me what we needed—and of course, I wasn't going to assassinate Mike to get his job at Berkeley—that I said, "The heck with it."

In quiet bitterness, I put away my masters' degrees, swallowed my love of working with athletes, quit my strength and conditioning role at Berkeley, and joined Sam in his medical sales business.

RED ZONE CHECK

1. The contact I had with FCA and the opportunity to bring twenty players to that FCA-hosted prayer breakfast ahead of the Holiday Bowl was just one example of how God showed me a glimpse of my future, though I didn't know He was doing so at the time. Has God ever foreshadowed something in your life, and only in hindsight, did you see what He had done? Perhaps it was an encounter with someone who came back into your life. Perhaps it was an experience or event. What does this say about God's providence? (John 13:7)

2. What do you make of my decision to find a higher paying career and walk away from a career that I loved (for a second time)—one where I felt I was making an impact? Have you ever faced a situation where you had to choose between something you wanted to do and something you felt like you "should" do? Where are the pressures from the "should" coming from? When faced with that kind of choice, how do you discern what God would have you do? (Luke 9:23)

Chapter 17

THE SACRIFICE

. . . the Bible sees GOD as the supreme good—not the individual or the family—and that gives us a view of marriage that intimately unites feelings AND duty, passion AND promise. That is because at the heart of the biblical idea of marriage is the covenant.

Tim Keller

My goals remained lofty.

By joining Sam's medical sales team, I hoped to earn enough money to not only support my family but also open my own gym to train athletes—much like what Dr. Marcus Elliott did when he founded P3. I even spoke with Marcus, and he supported the idea of building an offshoot of P3 in northern California that I could run. While we brainstormed, he told me the Lopez twins—Robin and Brook, the NBA players—could work out at my facility in the off-season since they lived in the area.

There was one hiccup, but it proved to be the only obstacle that mattered. I needed hundreds of thousands of dollars for the technology and equipment required to build the state-of-the-art center. Though I tried, I wasn't able to raise the additional money I needed to make it happen. Despite my disappointment, I fully trusted in God's sovereignty. He hadn't let me down before—ever.

My medical sales job took off, and I discovered I was good at it. We sold a strong, topical pain cream that used a cutting-edge delivery system to pass through the skin. I leaned into my outgoing personality and desire to help others as I met with countless doctors and built relationships that resulted in more sales. Within four months, I was the top salesperson in the company. For the next two years, I didn't lose that spot.

Kelly and I bought a house, and on the surface, all seemed to be going well. Though I liked and believed in the product I was selling, I didn't love what I was doing. Every fiber in my body, particularly my heart fibers, missed my coaching career. A byproduct of my longing to coach emerged. Resentment. Bitterness had crept in and ruled my mindset, perspective, and relationship with Kelly.

As all of this unfolded, Kelly and I started trying to have kids. The frequency and closeness of our physical intimacy over the years was not great, and the culmination of the bitterness I carried at having to leave coaching, Kelly's insecurities, and not experiencing success with getting pregnant right away strained our already fragile relationship.

Each negative pregnancy test crushed her. I felt sad, too, but for Kelly, it seemed her happiness was rooted in starting that family we had talked about. We visited fertility doctors, who could only tell us, "We don't know why you're not getting pregnant." The official diagnosis was *unexplained infertility.*

When I look back now, I see the grace of God in that diagnosis. There wasn't anything wrong with her eggs or my sperm. God knew what lay ahead for us. God was protecting us, steering the ship, turning ashes to beauty.

I didn't have the NFL spot. I didn't have a big college coaching job. The job in Hawaii had fallen through, and we had no children. He knew where I had been, what Kelly and I were going through, what I had sacrificed. In His omniscience, He knew every choice we'd make. He knew it all, and He was planning accordingly to draw me closer to Him. I firmly believe we have free will, but I also believe God has a grander plan that will prevail. He is sovereign. God was opening and closing doors to prevent more heartache and pain while ensuring I was positioned for what He wanted to do next in my heart.

Carrying the hopelessness that permeated our home, I looked for something to reignite my passion again. One night, while watching TV, I came across the CrossFit Games. Rich Froning Jr. was dominating. As I watched, I thought, *I think I can do that.* I found a CrossFit gym down the street from our house, and when I walked in for the first time, I told the owner and the primary trainer that my goal was to go to the CrossFit Games.

"Have you ever done CrossFit before?" the head coach at CrossFit San Ramon, Dusty Sulon, asked me through guarded eyes.

"No, but I'm athletic. I played pro football and also ran track and field in college. I know how to clean. I think I can learn this." What I didn't know was that Dusty was a regional CrossFit superstar that had never quite made it to the CrossFit Games, though he was an unbelievable athlete and had established a consistent training regime. When I learned this about him, I asked, "Okay. Can I train with you?"

Remember, I knew—had learned through my storied athletic career—that when you train with the best, when you're able to measure yourself against the most talented people around you, you can reach your own pinnacle. This is true in not only sports, but in work, life, and relationships.

In our first training session together, Dusty put me in my place. He included multiple difficult movements, all of what I had never done before. I think he wanted to teach me a lesson, to show me just how hard this CrossFit dream would be to accomplish. It worked; I was humbled.

I worked out at Dusty's gym—and with him—for one year, and he kicked my butt. He beat me in every imaginable way, from just being more fit to having more knowledge of the workouts, strategy, pacing—all the little tricks of the trade that made him a winner. With every defeat, I learned something about the sport and about myself. My passion for competition returned with a vengeance. I didn't just want to be good at CrossFit; I wanted to be great. That would require me to build my "engine," which consisted of a combination of anaerobic and aerobic maximum capacities, and master a variety of skills. I loved training with the goal of something to compete for, a prize at the end—to see the outputs of my commitment and work.

Within that first year, I improved by a large margin. Being almost 200 pounds and about six feet tall, I was considered big for CrossFit. The best athletes were five-foot-eight or nine, 185 pounds. That compact strength helps them through the smaller ranges of motion. But I didn't let my size impede my success. I had never done handstand push-ups before. I went from zero to over twenty in a row. I had never done muscle-ups before, and I increased my capacity from zero to ten or fifteen at a time. I had never snatched before, and that is where I made my hay. I started out only able to lift 135 pounds. As usual, I sought the best training and coaches I could find to get better, and a world-class facility, California Strength, was in my area. I got Olympic-level coaching from owner Dave Spitz and made huge improvements in a short period. Within a year, I snatched 225–245 pounds, then after eighteen months, I had improved to 275–280 pounds.

When I went to watch the Northern California CrossFit Regional in 2013, I saw a team running around called Combat Sports Academy

CrossFit (CrossFit CSA). They hailed from Dublin, California, only ten minutes away from Danville, where I lived. I hadn't heard of "team CrossFit" before that moment. I had been trying to qualify as an individual to make it to the CrossFit Games, but this idea of competing as a team intrigued me. The concept of being a part of a group again, one where the individuals share the load, felt right. Team members still need to be strong and have a high level of skill, but you can do shorter sets and tag a teammate in as you find little breaks that, sometimes, you don't get when you compete as an individual. So I strode over to the owner of CSA, a guy by the name of Kirian Fitzgibbons, and introduced myself.

Ironically, I had already signed up for a CrossFit event at CSA that was going to take place a couple of weeks later, and there, I did really well. So well that soon after the event, I received a call from Kirian . . .

"Josh, I'm impressed. I would love for you to come in and talk with me."

The first thing I noticed about Kirian's gym was the number of banners hanging on the walls. A friend of mine, who came to visit later, said something that I think describes the scene well: "They didn't leave any space for paint!" Banner after banner highlighted the gym's successes, not only in CrossFit but also in World Championships in combat martial arts, such as Muay Thai and Krav Maga—the latter a hand-to-hand self-defense system developed in Israel. CSA had certainly built a championship culture. I almost salivated.

Kirian brought me on to support his wife Jessica's CrossFit efforts and build a more powerful team (all teams are co-ed in CrossFit). I could snatch and clean more weight than anyone on their current squad, so I felt thrilled to have a role and provide something that the team needed.

A couple of years later, we brought in more strong guys, including Buddy Hitchcock and Tyler Cummings, to join the already talented group: phenom Dylan Macrae, the original captain Will Blaker, Brett Weidner, the most uplifting teammate Chris Connolly, former CrossFit games individual competitor Katie Hogan, Sarah Pierce, Ashley Rincon (a.k.a., Smashley), Alexys D'tiole, Brandy Bachmeyer, and CrossFit model and "It Girl," Jackie Perez. I spent several hours a day at the gym. I had trained by mind and body for my whole life, and after a long season away, this sport helped me feel great about myself again. I woke up at 4:30 in the morning to drive an hour to Manteca, California to train with Buddy Hitchcock—because again, I wanted to train with the best to give myself a viable chance to participate in the CrossFit Games. Buddy Hitchcock had been to multiple CrossFit Regionals as an individual competitor and almost made the games. He expanded on all the ways that Dusty used to push me and took that to another level.

During those few years, the divide between Kelly and me swelled deeper and wider. We both felt the continual disappointment of not being able to have children, and our time together grew limited with my busy schedule. On my side of the schism, I experienced disappointment with her lack of intimacy and the frigid conflict cycle that festered in our house, one we just couldn't seem to break free from or manage in a healthy way. Even when minor issues arose, she would withdraw into silence. Her disengagement would trigger feelings of rejection in me. This hurt reminded me of all my previous repudiation and often led to fear, which I covered with anger. I wanted to talk it out and would actively pursue reconciliation. When my attempts were rebuffed, I would respond with frustration and the cycle would begin again.

Marriage takes two people willing to give, and I wasn't perfect in that area either. For my part, I wasn't the most considerate husband. As one example, I wasn't helpful with cleaning the house. I wanted to clean my guts out for one Saturday every few weeks. She grew exasperated with living in a dirty house. Since then, I've learned to do a little at a time so the workload isn't so much and you're not living in any degree of mess all of the time. Other immaturities seeped through me into our relationship as well. I needed to grow up, but as a whole, our opposing conflict management styles and the lack of intimacy between us burdened our relationship more than anything else. We were both disheartened and desperately needed hope.

The more I turned to CrossFit, the more frequently came Kelly's accusations that I only wanted to go to the gym to look at "attractive, fit girls in little shorts." She couldn't be further from the truth. The real reason I spent so much time there was that I loved to compete. Competition and training my body for peak performance had always been my lifeblood goals (i.e., my idols). Admittedly, there are a lot of female athletes at CrossFit gyms that wear tiny shorts. To disrupt her paranoia and fears, I offered two solutions. First, I asked Kelly to go to the gym with me. She obliged for a month, but she loathed it. So she stopped going. Second, I asked if I could build my own home gym that would allow me to stay at the house to train. However, Kelly was frugal with finances, and that wasn't something she wanted to budget for.

After she nixed my ideas and offered none of her own, I continued to spend several hours at the gym, both in the mornings and in the evenings. I had found a place where I was appreciated, and I liked how I felt when I worked out. At one point, Kelly told me she hated the competitor in me, that the part of me that made me a warrior made her sick. When she saw me in "game mode," it made her physically nauseous. *Ouch.* Those words were a blow to my core. I had never felt so unseen or unloved for who I was, for how I viewed myself as an athlete *and* as a Christian man.

I am the youngest of six boys. We were trained by a father who played in the NFL and was a warrior of a man himself, a fierce competitor. I was raised to be a soldier for Christ first and foremost, *to fight the good fight* (2 Timothy 4:7), to be a strong, masculine male (but not toxic), and to fight for the woman I love and to further God's Kingdom.

> ***Be watchful, stand firm in the faith, act like men,*** **be strong.** ***Let all that you do be done in love*** **(1 Corinthians 16:13–14).**

And I still believe in all of those things. According to 1 Corinthians, a true man is vigilant, faithful, discerning of truth, brave in the face of opposition, tenacious through trials, and, like Christ, loving. I thought I was living that out. So when Kelly told me that the part of me that's the fighter was making her sick, it hurt my soul and stomped all over what I believed was my purpose in life.

Our marriage continued its downward spiral, and in hindsight, it's amazing and eye-opening how some things—fears, accusations, labels, negative mindsets, and more—can become self-fulfilling prophecies.

RED ZONE CHECK

1. God knows not only our choices but our futures, others' choices, and how everything fits together. He has all of the information we don't have. Have you ever been so narrowly focused on yourself that you've forgotten that God's grace and sovereignty take into account others' choices and lives too? Is this an eye-opening perspective—that it's not all about you? Why or why not? (Isaiah 46:10)

2. Have you ever been told that the core of what makes you *YOU* is not good enough—or worse, that it makes someone angry, sick to their stomach, or want to distance themselves from you? How does it feel? From my perspective, Kelly couldn't have chosen a worse part of me to dislike, to attack. As you reflect on how God has made you, what defines you? Who are you *really*? (Psalm 139:13–16)

   (Hint: To know what a true man is, you need to look no further than Jesus. He is the embodiment of manhood, the perfect example of what spiritual maturity looks like, which is our ultimate goal as men. Jesus lived in complete dependence on and obedience to the will of God while exemplifying the fruits of the Spirit, which are found in Galatians 5:22–23.) *Those same spiritual fruits are important for women to have as well. God gives us a wonderful picture of what a spiritually mature wife looks like in Proverbs 31.

Chapter 18

THE TEXTS

To love means loving the unlovable. To forgive means pardoning the unpardonable. Faith means believing the unbelievable. Hope means hoping when everything seems hopeless.
G.K. Chesterton

A self-fulfilling prophecy is the phenomenon where someone expects, fears, or predicts something, and this "prediction" seems to come true—simply because a person's later behavior aligns to fulfill that expectation, fear, or belief.

What Kelly accused me of in terms of liking the "girls in little shorts" is eventually what I became guilty of . . .

I wasn't getting the attention at home that I felt I deserved. I didn't feel loved or respected for who I was as a husband, let alone as a man. I'd given up two careers to satisfy Kelly's requirement that we stay in California and make the money we needed for the house we desired. I didn't feel wanted or attractive to my spouse, evidenced by her lack of initiating any physical touch and experiencing little responsiveness to my advances. I prayed for improved intimacy; I worked to achieve it, even seeking Christian counseling for us and doing everything I could to engage in this process, but it never happened.

Meanwhile, the CrossFit team movement was getting wise to the advanced strategies of recruiting stronger athletes from other places, and our gym started recruiting for and building our own super team, as it was called. One day, a female athlete came into the CSA gym. She had been a college soccer player, was athletic, and even though she didn't have any experience, she had a lot of potential—much like me when I had started out in CrossFit. She just needed to learn, and she was hungry to learn.

This female athlete worked out with me and several members of the team a few times. It was innocent at first because I had everyone's phone number, and sometimes, I would organize team training sessions. So when we exchanged numbers, I thought nothing of it.

Weeks later, one of my buddies and I went down to the CrossFit Games in Carson, just south of Los Angeles, for the third year in a row. The event was several days long, the environment incredible. The stadium was packed, and we watched Rich Froning Jr. and others dominate the Games. Energy high, I felt in my element . . . and happy. I thought, *I want to be here. I want to compete,* and my yearning to show what I was capable of intensified.

Nearly a week went by at the Games, and I spoke with Kelly on the phone every day. When it was time to drive home—a trip that normally takes five and a half hours—my friend's car overheated. After we fixed it, the trip ended up costing us a grueling eight hours. During the delay, I received a text from Kelly:

Why are you taking so long?

I explained our situation, but the fact I had no control over it didn't matter. Complaint after complaint came through my phone, including threats about leaving and going to her parents' house, which would have been a drive straight past me as my buddy and I made our way back. In essence, she was waiting for me to get back to take care of our pets so she could then leave.

One of the hardest parts of it all was that my friend was getting texts from his wife too. But they were the exact opposite in content and tone, explaining how she missed him and what she was going to do with him and to him when he returned. They playfully flirted back and forth, evidence of their love and desire for each other.

Meanwhile, Kelly continued to berate me. Sullen, trying to understand her reaction, and secretly wishing our relationship was as intimate and flirtatious as our friends' marriage, I sat in my buddy's car, mostly quiet as he drove us the rest of the way home.

Despite the text exchange, I was still excited to see Kelly when I got home. I had missed her. I was hoping for room to work things out, possibly for a night of connection and intimacy.

Kelly, I haven't seen you in a week. I'd like to be with you.

No, I'm tired. I have to get up early to go to my parents'.

This was just another check mark in the long line of rejections I had received from her. My face flushed, and my stomach clenched. I started making excuses, inwardly blaming her for all of our problems. God would show me later that my reaction was all about me . . . a reaction full of my flesh and my desires. But my reaction also indicated how I had felt in those moments. *Rejected. Unattractive. Unloved.*

The next day, after Kelly left for her parents, the new female athlete at the gym messaged me to say she had a CrossFit competition the following weekend and asked if I would help her get ready. I agreed.

Over the next several days, we trained and spent a lot of time together. It wasn't that I had *not* noticed that she was attractive before, but until then, I had ignored it. This girl was not only attractive, she was flirtatious. And I liked it. I realized pretty quickly that I liked feeling wanted and valued. I liked feeling attractive to someone. She *saw* me, and she gave me this kind of attention at a point in my life when I didn't feel seen by the one person in the world I wanted to be loved by most. Not only did this athlete get me, she *appreciated* my competitive nature. She even looked up to me. I was *someone* again.

And man, it felt good.

As the week went along, I started reciprocating the flirtatious engagement. But it stopped there. Nothing else happened. *Nothing.* I didn't cross any type of physical line, but I crossed an emotional one. I certainly wasn't protecting my wife, her heart, or our marriage by engaging in this kind of interaction with another woman.

Kelly returned home a week later, and I was in the shower when this female athlete started to text me. As before, it was openly flirtatious. Kelly read the text string . . . and it just broke her. I can only imagine how betrayed she felt at that moment. She waited for me to leave the house, on my way to a work appointment, then called me to confront me. I was ashamed, embarrassed. I hurt over the pain I could hear in her voice. When I returned from my work appointment, Kelly was gone. I had no idea where she had gone, and I was left alone in our house to contemplate what I had done and the potential ramifications of my actions.

There is no excuse for a married man, particularly one who is a follower of Christ, to open the door for a flirtatious relationship with someone who is not his wife. I want to make that clear. *I was wrong.* While I had done nothing "to cross a line" physically, my emotional tryst was absolutely sin. I had utterly failed at the fundamental calling that God entrusted to me as a husband and sacrificial leader. We are warned to flee from temptation and not to make provision for the flesh, and I did neither.

> *But I say to you that everyone who looks at a woman with lustful intent has already committed adultery with her in his heart* (Matthew 5:28).

After several days and with some prompting from others and me, she came back for a little while. The first days back turned into tenuous weeks, and a widening gap grew between us. In my flesh-stained mind, I felt justified for "wanting to be wanted" and appreciated for the warrior that I was and the breadwinner I had become. I looked at our house and thought about the sacrifices I had made to help us get it, and I felt frustrated with Kelly. I also felt bad, remorseful for the texts, but it wasn't the level of true repentance I should have had. I was still operating from my selfish nature. *Well, she's still not validating me in these ways . . .*

Halloween was approaching, and there was little change in our strained relationship, except for the addition of a new roommate to our home. I had hired my old friend, Blake Salter, to join my growing medical sales team. Blake had moved his entire life out to California to take a chance on building a career in the medical sales business. As I was paying part of his salary, training him, and trying to help him get on his feet, I offered him the chance to stay with Kelly and me for the first several months of his training period. No offense to Blake, but the timing could not have been much worse, considering the struggles that Kelly and I were already experiencing.

Additionally, in the early days of our friendship, Blake and I had been "partners in crime" as we hit the night scene in Orlando and Miami. So Kelly always had reservations about Blake and me reuniting for any "guys' nights."

The year before, I had attended a Halloween party at a doctor's house, whom I knew through my medical sales career. He was near the top financially, in terms of what he contributed to my business, since he wrote a significant amount of prescriptions for the product I sold. In the sales business, it's important to take advantage of opportunities to grow relationships, especially outside the office. I had invited Kelly to go, but she wasn't interested. And I had gone by myself.

This year, I was fired up to take Blake to the party, ready to have some fun. I hoped it would be a nice escape from the tense environment at home. I didn't formally invite Kelly this time. It was more of a "Hey, if you want to come, that's fine." Since it was work-related, she said no but told us to enjoy ourselves.

Two days before the Halloween party, the doctor canceled it. I already had approval to go out on Halloween, and Blake and I had been looking forward to wearing our costumes for a "guys' night out." I thought, *Shucks, what are we going to do now?* I didn't want to stay home and cancel the guys' night but also didn't really want to "third-wheel" it and make alternative plans to accommodate Kelly.

I heard an advertisement on the radio for a Halloween party in Sacramento that would have multiple rooms with different DJs. I invited Blake, who said, "Absolutely!" so I bought us tickets. Blake is not culpable for this decision at all—it was my choice not to tell Kelly that our plans had changed. She still thought we were going to the doctor's house.

Whatever messaging system I had set up with my devices, it turned out all of my texts came through on my iPad too. So while we were at this party, Blake and I got separated and sent texts to each other about what rooms we were in to try to find each other. Because of the lack of trust in our marriage, Kelly checked the iPad and discovered that we were not at the doctor's house. With her insecurities heightened, she checked my email—which I don't think was wrong, given my behavior—and found the receipt for the tickets for this party and realized I had lied.

Kelly said nothing for a couple of days. Instead, she waited until our next counseling session to set up a trap, to catch me in the lie in front of our counselor. When the trap was sprung, I was again ashamed and embarrassed, but I covered those feelings with anger. And in my anger, I yelled: "Stay the (explicative) out of my email!"

Kelly sat there in stunned silence and then started to cry. It was such a sad moment.

In Kelly's defense, there was more than one incident that broke the trust in our marriage, her trust in me. Aside from that flirtatious relationship with the woman at CrossFit, I went to an event that no married man should be at without his spouse—and lied about it. I wasn't drinking or doing drugs, but I wanted to be wanted and searching out opportunities to get that validation *from women that weren't my wife.* I had desperately wanted to feel free of the weight of the conflict in our relationship, and I did that by going to a Halloween party where women wore promiscuous costumes. I hadn't changed. My behavior had gotten worse in the time after the flirtatious text strings with the young woman at CrossFit.

The day after that explosive emotional counseling session, Kelly packed up and left while Blake and I were at work. I was terrified of where this would lead us. I asked Kelly to go back to the counselor with me as soon as possible. When we returned to counseling a few days later, the counselor set up a "trial separation" plan. This was not what I wanted or thought would give us the best chance to work on solving our issues together.

Kelly was certainly justified in terms of losing trust in me. I admit, I needed to change; my heart needed a transplant. But I didn't think Kelly should have left (and still don't). I firmly believe we could have worked on things together in our home, remaining united in covenant. We were both wounded and hurting. I would definitely have needed to earn back her trust and lead through action. But the best place to do that and demonstrate a change in heart would be in partnership, not separately. We needed more intervention, but with God, I believe we could have done it.

The Bible talks about not separating from your spouse, except for a time and by mutual agreement.

> *Do not deprive one another, except perhaps by agreement for a limited time, that you may devote yourselves to prayer; but then come together again, so that Satan may not tempt you because of your lack of self-control* (1 Corinthians 7:5).

While this verse talks about physical intimacy, I believe it applies to physical and emotional distance in marriage too. If couples separate temporarily, they should know when the separation is going to end, and it should be done to set each individual apart for the Lord. And, there should be every intention of coming back together in the united covenant. That's never what our separation was. Our counselor had advised us to have three weekly get-togethers during the separation: one date night, one business meeting (to talk about finances and life), and one counseling session.

Kelly and I didn't meet. I didn't see her again for months because she either blew off my attempts to set up meetings or didn't show up for them. She went to counseling by herself. And I went by myself. The worst part: there was no accountability for her to meet with me as the counselor advised. No one told her, "Kelly, you're not doing the things we all agreed on for this separation to work and for you two to come back together."

Just because I yelled and cursed and the room got tense for a minute did not mean there was any kind of abuse. My outburst was not kind or sweet or loving, and my tone was over the top. The use of profanity was wrong, but it wasn't part of a larger pattern of abuse. She didn't need to be "evacuated from the home" for her safety, as it seemed was happening.

I wondered, *How are we ever going to grow back together?* Our counselor had no answers, so I stopped seeing him. I asked Kelly if she would consider talking with Don and Sally Meredith or even another local counselor—someone we could both trust—but she refused. I even bought us plane tickets to the Merediths' city to show how dedicated I was to working things out. She still refused. She did write Don and Sally Meredith a ten-page letter, blasting me and telling them about all of my failures. Kelly wasn't wrong regarding most of my failures, but her perspective leveled the blame squarely on me. The last paragraph summed up everything well:

"Josh thinks the problems we have are just normal problems that couples can work through during the rest of their lives together. That may be true for him, but that is no longer true for me. I'm moving on with my life."

She was moving on with her life . . .

While I am forever culpable for my mistakes, one of the defining factors, I think, in Kelly's decision to leave me permanently was the advice our counselor gave us, which in hindsight, I find to be unprofessional, especially if a couple is seeking healthy relationship recovery. The problems Kelly and I had—they were not things that were insurmountable. Conflict management and intimacy issues drive couples apart, but couples can work through them if they choose to do so. That counselor's advice, which gave her the excuse to leave, sealed the deal. In my opinion, we had found the counselor Satan would have wanted us to see, even though we were grown adults making our own choices. God implores us in His word to seek counsel, which I still strongly encourage others to do. But it is imperative that this counsel be rooted in godly truth and that there be evidence of that in the life of your counselor. Worldly wisdom can only take you so far; without God, it all leads back to a place of sin and self-reliance.

The months dragged on as winter turned to spring, and I waited to hear from her. A darkness seemed to swallow me as I wondered what was happening. I stopped going to church, angry with God for letting this situation continue. The marriage was essentially over. Kelly wrote that she was moving on to the Merediths. She wasn't engaged in any conversation, and we hadn't done anything toward resolution. I felt more hopelessness with each passing month. We were stuck in some strange limbo, me feeling like I was being held hostage by her silence and all of the unknowns—*if* or *when* I would be served with divorce paperwork. It was more like purgatory. I eventually got to the place where I considered us divorced in my mind and heart. I felt abandoned and gave up hope that we could reconcile.

> *The heart is deceitful above all things, and desperately sick; who can understand it?* (Jeremiah 17:9)

Lonely and broken, I said, "The heck with it." I sent a private message to a female acquaintance through Instagram, explaining I was not officially divorced but separated from my wife. Then I asked her if she was interested in getting together for coffee. What I was really saying was, "God, I don't trust you. I don't feel valued, loved, or wanted. I want companionship, and I'm going to take care of this myself." Though I felt abandoned and hopeless, it doesn't mean that was the reality. Our feelings are *not* objective truth. Only God knows what is true. He is truth; He alone defines truth. My tattered heart, just like all of our sinful, compromised compasses, could not discern truth apart from Christ.

Unbeknownst to me, through all that time of silence, Kelly had been monitoring my Instagram account. She was watching. Waiting. Hoping, I'm sure, to see if I'd change. She was assessing my choices. And what she saw was me choosing to dive deeper into CrossFit, spending hours every day with teammates, including the "girls in little shorts." Kelly was looking for evidence that she was important to me, a priority even. And I didn't give her any indication that I was changing my choices or my priorities. The direct message on my social media was the straw that broke her heart in two.

I had forsaken the wife of my youth.

Let your fountain be blessed, and rejoice in the wife of your youth (Proverbs 5:18).

Only hours after I sent that DM on Instagram, I received a text message from Kelly: *It's over, I'm going to file for divorce.* In the months since she had left, I had contemplated many times the possibility that it might be over. But this text hit hard, the words staring me right in the face; my worst fears had just become a reality. I had a flood of emotions overwhelm me in that moment, but the three that stand out are fear, sorrow, and desperation. I was terrified that my life with Kelly was indeed over, and I was racked with guilt and conviction that I had caused it. I became desperate to do anything I could to change it.

I had learned Kelly was staying with one of my old CrossFit buddies and his wife. Immediately after receiving her text message, I hopped in my car and raced over with the hope of talking to her and finding any sliver of hope to save our marriage. My *former* friend answered the door shirtless and told me to leave. I could see Kelly weeping through the upstairs bedroom window. My wife was just a few feet away from me, hurting, and there was nothing I could do to get to her, to fix it.

Still despondent, I tried to go to her job the next day, waiting in the parking lot and hoping to catch her after work. As I sat in my car, I received a call from the Merediths. "Josh, Kelly called us. She went out the back door . . . she's already left; you gotta go home." Don and Sally prayed with me, helping me through that horrific moment, as I wept in my car.

You keep track of all my sorrows. You have collected all my tears in your bottle. You have recorded each one in your book (Psalms 56:8).

God keeps track of every one of our tears. He knows exactly what you are going through, and He cares more than we can imagine. But at that moment, I didn't feel loved or seen. I felt the searing pain of despair and more than anything, I felt alone.

Weeks later, Kelly agreed to meet with me face to face at a Starbucks. As I drove up to the parking lot, after not having direct contact with her now for many months, I pondered the gravity of this encounter. I knew it would likely be the last time I'd see her, and I trembled. I sat in my car as the tears welled underneath my lower lids.

I was trying to pull myself together, as I wanted to be composed in that potential final meeting. I prayed to God to give me the words to say, to carry me through this. I knew I didn't have it inside me to deal with this. In the middle of my prayer, softly in the background I could hear a song playing. I had left my radio on and didn't realize it until that moment. A song I had never heard before reached through the airwaves to touch my heart. It was Kari Jobe's "I Am Not Alone," and I knew—I could feel the Holy Spirit speaking to me—that in the shadow of the valley, I need not fear because God was with me. I was *not* alone. I knew in my soul that He saw me. *I always see you, Josh.* Again, I wept, feeling His loving arms wrap around me. Despite my sin and selfishness, He had not abandoned me. God steadied me, and when I entered that coffee shop, Kelly and I were able to talk amicably about the divorce and start to divide our assets. We ended up having a few more conversations like that over the next several months.

Jesus Christ lived in the flesh, experienced every human emotion, and was tempted just as we are, and yet, He did not sin. But Christ being without sin doesn't make Him empathize with us any less. He loves us in the midst of our sin, right in the deepest darkest depths of it. He went to the cross for us while we were still drowning in it. But He also wants to set us free. He wants to change us.

In my loneliest and hardest hours, I had sinned. I became the person any of us can become if we neglect to surrender to the Holy Spirit inside us. It didn't happen overnight. The man that I had become wasn't one I recognized. As I entered into my wedding vows six years before, there was no way I would have imagined that I would ever be capable of these selfish decisions. Through my young adulthood, I had stood for something. I had abstained from drinking alcohol or doing drugs, from premarital sex, and I had convinced myself that I was strong. That I was somehow righteous. I would never have said that, but that's how my prideful heart felt. It is said that pride goes before a fall. Indeed, I had given in to my deceitful heart, and the truth is, apart from Christ, I am not good. None of us are. God gives to us because He is *good* and He is full of *grace,* not because we are deserving.

Within this season of my story, in these moments of despair and hopelessness, is where God gets ahold of my heart *again.* He always wants our broken, repentant, submitted hearts. It's where He does His best work. You do not have to change to receive the gift of salvation, but if you have legitimately submitted your life to Him, You *will* change.

Amid the pain, He showed up, like He always did and always will. He showed me I needed to give my whole life to Him—*everything.* I hadn't done that yet. I thought I had with the football sacrifices and closed doors, with the coaching career changes, and by trying to move Jacob's story forward in California, but the truth was, my heart had not been completely transformed yet. God wanted it all . . . and he was going to get it all.

RED ZONE CHECK

1. Research has tied the self-fulfilling prophecy to relationships. Our expectations about the successes and failures in our relationships can influence their outcomes. How might this have played a role in Kelly's and my marriage? Have you experienced this or witnessed this in any relationships in your life? (Hebrews 11:1–2)

2. There's nothing wrong with having the emotional needs to be accepted, valued, respected, and even desired. These needs, created and supplied by God and those He appoints in our lives, can propel us forward in tough situations and produce a level of self-confidence that we all strive for in our personal and professional lives. But there's a narrow line dividing healthy, God-given assurance and our stubborn egos motivated by our sin-filled flesh. A big indicator we're on the wrong side is when we act against our own values—and God's plan—to soothe our suffering. It's especially difficult to admit we're wrong when the person we've hurt is treating us unkindly, unfairly, or engaging in behaviors that have hurt us too. Have you been there? What happened? Did you find grace? Were you able to give grace to the person who offended you? (2 Corinthians 12:9, Hebrews 12:15)

Chapter 19

THE DARK THANKSGIVING

Adversity is not simply a tool. It is God's most effective tool for the advancement of our spiritual lives.
Charles Stanley

How quickly we forget how God shows up for us in the darkness, the ways He carries us when we can no longer stand. The human heart is prone to wander and not toward God.

In the months after that Starbucks meet-up with Kelly, the hole in my heart, which I had tried to fill through my own means grew larger. The initial shock of being left and our upcoming divorce was turning to bitterness.

God had forsaken me, allowing—possibly causing—the darkest season of my life.

Or so my twisting emotions had convinced me.

Blake, still living with me, was struggling with some things too—namely loneliness. He was homesick, and his medical sales were spotty, which caused him to be hard on himself. The only friend Blake had in

California was me, and I wasn't my normal, positive self, given what I was going through. As the Thanksgiving holiday approached, he learned he couldn't make it back home, which only added to his darkness.

As Blake fought off loneliness, I wrestled with God. Hot anger coursed through me, fully directed at Him. Operating from a false narrative, I believed that because I had been so good, I deserved more from God than a broken marriage. "God, I served You! I never drank alcohol—not even a drop—never did drugs, remained a virgin until I was married, stayed active in the Church, started an FCA group at Pierce College, and initiated a coach's Bible study at Cal Berkeley. Yet here I am, thirty-five years old, and my wife has left me!" I spit my list of righteous deeds at Him.

When Thanksgiving Day arrived, Blake and I slept until almost noon. When I emerged from my bedroom cave, I entered an even bleaker house. The shades were still pulled down over the windows. No lights pierced the darkness, and the air was stale. I opened the refrigerator and found no food. When Blake woke up, we sat and watched TV, commiserating in silence. Eventually, hunger pangs stirred our morose postures, and we ventured out to find a restaurant that was open. The only thing we could find was Subway. I have nothing against a delicious foot-long sub, but that was not an ideal Thanksgiving meal. As we feasted on our subs, I battled two warring thoughts:

I can't believe Kelly left me, and I can't believe I'm eating a sub for Thanksgiving.

I'm grateful Blake is here. At least, we have each other.

Despite finding something to be grateful for, bitterness seeped through my pores. I didn't know how I had gotten to this point, this dark place of separation and divorce. I just couldn't fathom it; it felt like a nightmare, an alternate reality. All I wanted to do was wake up.

For the next couple of months, I shook my fist at God. "I did what I thought You wanted me to do!" I screamed. I had assumed my marriage would be blessed because I had done all of the "right things" leading up to it.

I had been the person leading Bible studies and facilitating FCA groups. I had grown up in the Church and tried so hard to live a pure life—free from premarital sex . . . drugs and alcohol too. So I thought I had somehow *earned* the joy of being loved well by my wife. I assumed our marriage would be a success, that I'd be treated the way I always imagined and adored by my wife. My heart was torn, realizing I had made mistakes but also confused by how my life was unfolding. My deceitful heart convinced me I had earned more, that I had done everything I could to live "rightly." That I never *deserved* any of this. This notion of *deserving* always gets us in trouble with God and in our own spirits. Much like the older brother in the story of the prodigal son (Luke 15:11–31), we feel owed and don't *really* want a relationship with the Father. We just want the stuff he can give us. This was my sinful mindset, and God would soon reveal this to me.

I continued to lament my current state and why it all should have worked. I had chosen Kelly for all the "right reasons" in my mind's eye. Kelly was a beautiful woman with an amazing heart. But I had other opportunities to choose a different kind of mate in my young dating life. There had been cover models and actresses and high-level athletes, but I realized they weren't as sold out for God as I would have wanted in a spouse, many of them placing beauty and celebrity careers—their vanity—ahead of God. I wanted a pat on the back from God for my great choice. I had chosen a woman who worked as a speech pathologist, one who helped kids. She loved serving people—a tender-hearted girl, as Don Meredith had confirmed. Kelly had also been raised in a good Christian family. She had all the things a Christian man might want to choose in a life partner. I thought I was "living right." That word, *right,* stoked my anger. For my whole life, I had done everything right! I was a good person! From the outside looking in, everything looked right and good . . . yet it didn't work out. I couldn't hold our marriage together. Resentment, guilt, and shame enveloped me, and I turned it all toward God in bitter agony.

In that dark season, I asked, "Who am I now?" I'd lost football, coaching, and then my marriage. All joy had been stripped from my life, and I didn't know the way out. There was no light. Only darkness.

I wondered if I would ever date again. If I did, I wondered if I'd keep my covenant regarding pre-marital sex. After all, I was no longer a virgin. I questioned if I'd still make the biblical choice to abstain. I knew that was what God would direct me to do, but my anger clouded my judgment. Of course, I know now, as I look back, the point was (and is) not about maintaining perfection in any given area of our lives. But it's about our heart position, about submitting everything to God and His perfect design. I'm in no way diminishing the importance of waiting until marriage to engage in sexual intimacy. I'm saying that a heart that is fully submitted to Christ will want to do things in His timing, not ours. But my heart had been deceived. The truth is that everything is His, including our sexuality; the only things we hold are our choices.

> *For by him all things were created: things in heaven and on earth, visible and invisible, whether thrones or powers or rulers or authorities; all things were created by him and for him. He is before all things, and in him all things hold together* (Colossians 1:16–17).

As I raged, I withheld myself from God. I didn't want to go back to the church where everyone knew Kelly and me as a couple. I tried to keep in touch with the young couple who led our small group Bible study from our former church, Robert and Jenna. I knew they cared about both of us and loved the Lord first and foremost. They stayed in contact with me but also with Kelly, and that hurt too. Part of me hoped Jenna would call Kelly out and say divorce wasn't the right path. That she'd convince Kelly it wouldn't honor God and encourage her to change her mind. I think Jenna challenged Kelly to reconsider, but Kelly's mind was set. Her choice was made.

While I stopped attending church services and events, I didn't stop believing in God. Despite my rage against God, He never stopped loving me and gently drew me to Himself. God never went anywhere; I was the one, through my sin and rebellion, who drove a wedge between us. But His great love for me and desire for a deeper relationship would not let go of me.

One day in the spring of 2015, I found myself sitting at Cornerstone Fellowship Church in Livermore, California. It's a megachurch with five locations, thousands of members. I don't even remember how I got there. But that day, a miraculous appointment unfolded . . .

Cornerstone Fellowship Church had a lead pastor, Steve Madsen, who preached a majority of the time. They would live stream his sermons to all of the locations. But that day, they did something different. At the campus I attended, they had invited an associate pastor, Matt Warner, to preach, something he did only a few times per year.

Matt would later tell me that on that Sunday, he felt called to preach about something he had never talked about publicly from the pulpit: his divorce. There is a stigma in many churches surrounding divorce, and he felt compelled to address it. *That day.*

As I sat in the congregation, Matt preached about how divorce is not God's design but how He can use divorce for His glory. He spoke about how a broken marriage is never God's will—rather it's born from human sin, choices, and dysfunction—but God allows it because of the hardness of men's hearts. In His omniscience and glory, God can use our sin for His divine purpose. Surrounded by thousands in that worship center, I wept. My soul knew God had orchestrated this sermon especially for me. I am sure many others were touched by Matt's words that day, but God knew I *needed* them. As Matt spoke, it was as if God was reaching through the ceiling, through my pain, and saying, "Josh, I still see you. I haven't left you. You have walked away from me, but I haven't gone anywhere. I'm right here."

Afterward, I made my way down to the stage and thanked Matt for his transparent story. I shared that it was my story too. He asked me if I was meeting with anybody to talk through the pain. "Yeah. I mean, I talk to my parents. I get counsel . . ."

"Well, I'd love to meet with you if you want to talk more," he offered.

"Yeah. I'd like that."

After that God-ordained day, every Wednesday morning at 7:30 a.m., Matt Warner and I met for breakfast at Starbucks. He'd ask questions; I'd talk. He'd listen. We both cried. He encouraged me by just being there and caring, and he'd sometimes talk about his experience with his divorce. This kind of fellowship was exactly what the Bible says about how to support one another through hardship.

> *Bear one another's burdens, and so fulfill the law of Christ* (Galatians 6:2).

Matt sat with the broken-hearted—me. He lifted me up week after week. Then, after a few months of listening to my sob story, he challenged me. He asked me to open my Bible to Ephesians 5. We read the whole chapter, which I would encourage you to do too. But his focus for me that day was on this section:

> *Husbands, love your wives, as Christ loved the church and gave himself up for her, that he might sanctify her, having cleansed her by the washing of water with the word, so that he might present the church to himself in splendor, without spot or wrinkle or any such thing, that she might be holy and without blemish. In the same way husbands should love their wives as their own bodies. He who loves his wife loves himself* (verses 25-28).

"Josh, is there anywhere in this passage that says your love for Kelly is, in any way, dictated by what she does? Or by how she acts?"

I perked up a little. "No."

I instantly saw where Matt was going, and I tried to submit to the humility required to own it. Matt continued, "Did you talk to Kelly harshly?"

"Yeah, but she . . ."

"Did you disrespect her at any time?"

"Yeah, but she . . ."

"Josh, you keep saying, 'yeah, *but.*' God calls us to be leaders, and there is no *yeah, but* in that call. How we love our wives is not based on their performance or their reactions or their behaviors."

This ground-breaking insight pierced me, and godly sorrow gripped me. I grieved over my sin, my part in all of it. The next thing Matt said solidified everything. "How would you describe the love that Christ showed His Church?"

"Sacrificial," I answered in a near whisper.

"Would you say that your love for Kelly looked like that?"

I didn't have to say anything more. We both knew the answer. I had justified my behaviors, my opinions, and what I had done over the years. Yet there was no justification for any of it. I had sinned against God and against my wife, and I needed to repent. Fresh tears sprung forth. There are a lot of tears in this chapter because there was a lot of pain to acknowledge and much sin to reconcile in my life. I cried in that Starbucks because I knew I had been wrong. The Holy Spirit convicted me right there in front of my cup of coffee.

I had felt so righteous in the separation and divorce. Even though I had engaged in inappropriate flirting and those text strings—and admitted that was wrong—I had still believed Kelly was at fault. I thought she had driven me to it, and I used her lack of intimacy, how she shelled up during conflict, that she would run away from communication, how she didn't support my career, and how I never felt encouraged by her . . . I used all of her choices and behaviors as my ammunition. I had compiled all of these reasons for why I had done what I did, why I felt how I felt, and believed it had all been justified. But I was completely wrong. Ephesians 5 showed me that I needed to own it—every ounce of it. Own all the ways in which I had sinned against God, failed to lead and protect my wife, and hurt her.

I hadn't led sacrificially, as Christ does. My love for Kelly was not unconditional. It was very much based on performance. When she didn't give me what I desired or felt like I so righteously deserved, I withheld from her or selfishly did whatever I wanted to do to meet my own needs. Worst of all, I didn't lead her toward Christ. I wasn't fully devoted to Him. I wasn't sold out for Him. That was evident in my life, and she could see it and sense it every day.

A lack of submission to Him is the ultimate sin and shows a true lack of love for Him and trust. So, ultimately, I had failed in pretty much every way a husband can at the primary responsibilities God had entrusted me with, and that truth felt crushing.

I asked Kelly to meet with me one more time before our divorce was going to be final in January 2016. She agreed to see me in a public park. Once I was in front of her, I got on my knees. "Kelly, I was wrong. Everything is on the table in terms of my job or CrossFit . . . I'll stop everything. I'll stop competing. I'll do anything." As the grass dug into my knees, I admitted my selfishness and told her what Matt had walked me through. Opening my Bible, I showed her the verses in Ephesians 5.

"Why couldn't you have seen this years or even months ago?"

"I can't go back and fix what I've done. God has finally gotten me to this place. I can't make up for the past, but I can move forward and be the man and husband that He made me to be." I asked her if she'd consider dropping the divorce and dissolving the paperwork.

Kelly asked for time to ponder everything. I knew it was a lot to consider. A couple of days later, Kelly texted me. She would proceed with the divorce. But regardless of her decision, I had been humbled before God. I was doing what He called me to do, and my heart was finally in the right place. I was repentant and truly able to own my sin in it all.

RED ZONE CHECK

1. Have you been convicted and experienced the godly sorrow I describe in this chapter? A time when another Christ-follower perhaps called you out, in truth and in love, and your eyes and heart were opened to that truth? How did you feel? Did you repent, change course, never look back? Did you fight it? Share your story with someone else. (2 Corinthians 7:10)

1. We all have moments when we feel God is talking straight to us. We could be in a room full of thousands, but we just know God is prompting us, speaking to us, or comforting us. He is a relational God and made us for fellowship with Him. Describe your relationship with God. Is it intimate? Honest? Deep? Do you feel seen? Heard? Valued? Or could it use some work on your part? Describe a time when God reached through the ceiling for you. (Revelation 3:20)

Chapter 20

THE ASK

You don't have to go to heathen lands today
to find false gods. America is full of them.
Whatever you love more than God is your idol.
Dwight L. Moody

Months went by, and Matt continued to pour into my spiritual well-being. Eventually, I felt healthy enough to give back and serve, but I wasn't sure in what way, shape, or form. I only knew I could trust God to point me to His path. Matt suggested I lead a high school life group at Cornerstone Church. Basically, it was a small group Bible study for teens that met once per week. First, he said, I'd have to talk with the high school ministry leader, Clint Rutledge.

Clint and I met for breakfast, and I shared the different parts of my story that had led me to the café table where we sat. The conversation felt right, anointed even. Soon after, I became one of the high school life group leaders—paired with John Lombardi, who was the head of the young adult ministry at the church.

Not only did John and I lead together, we grew together as friends too. We went to the movies and worked out together, and that led to me hanging out with some of the other pastors and leaders at the church. God was surrounding me with a strong network of men who loved the Lord and had devoted their lives to Him. God used those leaders to refine the parts of me that were still prone to wander.

Six months later, Clint approached me. "Josh, we're doing a sermon series on how to share your testimony. We're asking different people from the church community to participate. Would you be willing to share your God-story with the students? You've just been so transparent—"

Before he had finished the request, I answered. "Absolutely."

In front of over two hundred high school students, I shared my testimony, the pieces of my life's puzzle that had driven me, at times consumed me, and finally prepared me to accept the abundant life God had for me. I spoke about my experience with that high school football camp, the various career changes, and my divorce. I laid it all bare.

Afterward, Clint approached me. "That was amazing, Josh! Thank you. Hey, would you consider speaking at FCA groups? They meet at high schools everywhere. I really think your story resonates with this age group."

I smiled and repeated my answer from before. "Absolutely!" I saw God's hand in these steps, leading me to someplace new, somewhere filled with purpose. And I couldn't wait to find out where.

For the next couple of months, from early 2016 into the spring of that year, I traveled to several high schools to offer my testimony and a message for the kids. Northern California FCA Director Clay Elliott attended a few of these huddles. There was one particular huddle that made a significant impact on me. I had not delivered the best talk that day. My message was disjointed, and I believed it had fallen flat. Afterward, Clay used a few minutes to offer a gospel presentation, reminding the three dozen students of some of the things I had mentioned. When he gave the students the opportunity to respond to God's call, I was skeptical. *These kids are not going to respond,* I thought. *I wasn't on my A-game today, and I'm not sure how many of these kids just showed up for free pizza.*

I could not have been more wrong. Five kids raised their hands. They had decided to give their lives to Jesus. They were moved to *respond.* I was floored.

God showed me He can use anything and anyone at any time to reach hearts. The power of the Holy Spirit showed me I was making God too small. I was reminded . . . it's not about me. Yes, we have the responsibility to be prepared, give an account of why we believe, do our homework, routinely be in God's Word, and pray. Once we do all of that, once we relent to the *sweet pursuit* of the Holy Spirit, God can and will work mighty miracles.

Clay asked me to lunch after that perspective-changing huddle. He said he was impressed with my testimony and how vulnerable I was with the kids. "Josh, would you consider coming on FCA staff?" he asked. I didn't know what that meant. What I did know was I loved to speak to groups, particularly this age group. I knew with this form of evangelism, on these public-school campuses, I felt immense purpose, value, and responsibility as I shared God's Word. I felt like I was *in the zone*—a sports term, but just as relevant in this case too.

> *As each has received a gift, use it to serve one another, as good stewards of God's varied grace* (1 Peter 4:10).

"What does being on staff entail?" I asked. "How do I get paid?"

Clay explained that much like missionaries, I would have to raise my own support and the funds needed to run the programs, organize and facilitate the huddles, buy the food and the t-shirts, and pay for the camps.

"Clay, I appreciate it. But no, that's not for me."

He asked me to pray about it, and I shook my head. I knew what that would mean. I jokingly call that request—to pray about something—the "kiss of death ask." In reality, it's a blessing from the Lord. *Pray about it?* At that point, I had a strong intuition of what would happen.

Nonetheless, I prayed about it, and much like Paul, praying for the Church of Ephesus, I asked:

> *. . . that the God of our Lord Jesus Christ, the Father of glory, may give [me] a spirit of wisdom and of revelation in the knowledge of him, that [I] may know what is the hope to which he has called [me], what are the riches of his glorious inheritance in the saints* (Ephesians 1:17–18, adjusted as personal prayer).

I also consulted with Don and Sally Meredith, my parents, and some close friends. They all told me that my background and the gifts that God has given me align well with the FCA mission. They also emphasized that if this was God's will, He would make a way. He would provide. I knew God was confirming His will in multiple ways. And I thought, *Yup. I'm doing this.*

A few weeks later, I took the onboarding steps and went through the training to start at FCA that upcoming school year, in the fall of 2016. There were books to read and online courses to complete. Meanwhile, I was still doing medical sales as my primary job, and I remained heavily involved in CrossFit—having just competed in another CrossFit Regional in May—and still worked out several hours a day.

It's true: CrossFit was still ruling my world. Being an athlete, relishing the competition, and training my body to be the strongest and fastest it could be continued to shape my identity, as it had since I was a teenager.

Through CrossFit, the athlete in me had been reborn after giving up football all those years ago. Once Kelly left, CrossFit became an even bigger part of my life, and I was working out six hours per day while working full time in medical sales. No longer finding my identity as a husband, and no longer attending church after Kelly left, I looked to my success in athletics to fill the void, pouring out my frustration through my zealous workouts. It was much like how I had channeled my frustration into tackling all those years ago in football. *Crazy White.*

My first team CrossFit Regional experience in 2014 was full of thrilling highs and crushing lows. On the first day of competition, I hit a huge 260-pound hang snatch, the second-largest lift of anyone in the competition, and it helped give us a top five finish. Unfortunately, one of my teammates got extremely sick that night and did everything he could just to get out on the floor so we wouldn't be disqualified. It wasn't the finish we hoped for or expected, but it stoked my appetite to come back stronger the next year and make it to the games.

Our work was cut out for us. So I woke up at 4:30 a.m. daily and drove over an hour to train with Buddy Hitchcock—who became one of my best friends—to have him kick my butt regularly. Because of that dedication, I got better and better, and our team got closer and closer to that goal of qualifying.

That next year, in 2015, the rules changed, and we could recruit from outside of our area or gym to form what people called a "Super Team." I brought in Buddy, and our team became a true powerhouse.

We earned the second best score in the open tournament in the Northern California Region. We were going into the Regional confident that we'd make it to the CrossFit Games. Unfortunately, we ended up narrowly missing the mark—by just a few pounds and a couple of seconds. If I had lifted ten more pounds or a teammate been a few seconds faster in one event, we would have made it. Each of us felt the heartbreak. To be so close . . .

The following year, Buddy told us he wasn't going to travel down to our facility to compete with us. Financially, he couldn't make it work between the gas money and missing too many opportunities to teach classes at his gym. So I recruited other teammates—Tyler Cummings and April Gemein—who were phenomenal athletes. But our team didn't make it past the Northern California Regional again in 2016 either.

Buddy had been drafted by a spin-off league created by a CrossFit higher-up, Tony Budding, called The GRID League. It was a professional sport league of CrossFit that featured co-ed, tag-team races with heavier weights, more complicated movements, and a new format. With my strengths, I was well suited for GRID because most of the races would last only two or three minutes. They were relay-style races where you go in, empty your tank, and tag out.

Buddy had tried to talk me into going to the try-outs back in 2014, but Kelly hadn't left me yet. I knew as a married man that I wouldn't have the time to commit to a professional sport while also working a full-time job. But in 2015, Kelly was gone, and GRID was taking off, even occasionally airing on NBC Sports. I had watched a GRID match at Cal–Berkeley. It was amazing to see it, and I decided I wanted to do it.

It was another level, another way, for me to secure my identity as a professional athlete. To apply, I had to film myself completing the movements and submit an online application. The GRID decision-makers scored the applicants against each other, and when I checked my results, I had some great scores. They invited me to the GRID combine in the Bay Area, held at CrossFit Pleasanton.

It was an incredible weekend. There were no team captains, so to speak, but our team's coach put me in a leadership position. I was chosen to anchor the final movement of the final race of the match, which would decide the winner. The task set before me was to complete twenty-five thrusters at ninety-five pounds. When I was tagged into the race by my teammate, my competitor from the other team was already on the bar and four or five reps into the movement—a large margin. My brain screamed at my body, knowing I had to make up those four or five reps in less than twenty-five chances. It was the end of two days of grueling workouts and races, and my body was already tired. However, I pushed any thoughts of fatigue or defeat from my head, and I jumped on the bar, primed to go as fast as I could.

Through my breaths, I heard the announcers giving the audience the play-by-play. "Josh Phillips is now only three reps behind! . . . Phillips is now only two reps behind!" I willed my body to go faster. I went full-send mode. ". . . Josh Phillips caught him! . . . He's passed him!!!"

I had won. I thought of Vince Lombardi's famous quote: "If winning isn't everything, why do they keep score?" Man, it felt good—the double hit of the "joy hormones," dopamine and serotonin, to my brain.

I was invited to go to the main combine (the final, national try-outs) in Baltimore, Maryland. The league put me up in a hotel, and I had another great weekend of competition. One event was called the Echo Races. It's a combination of several movements, bodyweight gymnastics and heavy barbells, some of the same movements as in CrossFit but in a set order raced twice, back-to-back. And you don't get to make any substitutions between these two races. Teams set their roster and go with whomever they've selected and despite whatever happens. Smack in the middle of the line-up, our team noted there were fifteen muscle-ups to be completed on the gymnastics rings.

Now, fifteen is not that many for a man to do these days, even unbroken (all in a row). But there weren't many people doing fifteen unbroken muscle-ups, especially not back-to-back, which is how GRID had it set up. Every other team in the combine split up the reps between two athletes, each doing seven or eight and then tagging the next person. I volunteered to do them.

"Okay. How many?" they asked as they looked around to find another athlete to split the reps with me.

"I've got the muscle-ups—all of them," I said.

By any standards, I was not gigantic for a CrossFitter at around six feet, 197 pounds. There are certainly bigger and stronger athletes. But the specific role I was trying to fill in GRID was as the utility athlete, strong enough to move heavy barbells but proficient enough at gymnastics to cycle those movements quickly. Here was my opportunity to show that I could knock out thirty muscle-ups in just a couple of minutes and show my value. My combine teammates looked at me skeptically, especially Wes Kitts, who had taken the responsibility of doing our team's heavy barbell movement. Kitts looked like a big, strong guy, but I had no idea who he was at the time. He is now an Olympian, Pan American Games Champion, and record-holder in Olympic weightlifting. My bravado to take on the muscle-ups drew a raised eyebrow, but I gave Wes a confident nod. I loved the feeling of the pressure to get the job done and, praise God, I delivered. Our team won both Echo Races and those precious seconds I shaved off by not being subbed out made the difference.

After the combine, the GRID League held a draft. On draft day, I waited by my phone, similar to many years before at Yale, when I waited for that NFL phone call. But this time, the phone rang, and I was selected in the seventh round of 2015 by the LA Reign. Vindication! I had been unsure if I would get drafted at all, but had hoped I might get picked by my local San Francisco Fire and get to join Buddy Hitchcock again. But I was elated to finally hear my name called and get to join the likes of Noah Olsen (who finished second in the CrossFit Games), Kenneth Leverich, Kristin Clever, Lindsay Valenzuela, and so many other amazing athletes.

What an incredible blessing. This fed my ego like nothing had in a long time. My medical sales boss, Sam, gave me permission to go, so I traveled to the GRID training camp down in LA, lived in a house they rented for us, and enjoyed the CrossFit life 24/7. The validation this provided me was like nothing else. *Look, everyone. I'm a real athlete again.*

I knew I could do it.

That first year of GRID, I had been the last guy to make the team when they announced the roster. The next day, the GRID League announced brand-new races and new movements. One of the movements involved lifting a gigantic D-ball, a 200-pound medicine ball. Athletes had to pick it up and throw it over their shoulders or throw it over a box. One of the guys I had beat out to make the active roster was a six-foot-six, 255-pound beast named Cameron Frazier, an enormous and strong dude. I had done the bodyweight movements better than him; he wasn't able to rep them as fast as me. But Cam was a specialist, and I was a multi-purpose athlete, just like Noah and Kenny. We didn't have another specialist to pick up that ball, so Cam, with his long arms and giant frame, was pulled up, and I basically got benched. *Again.*

Yet again, injustice had caught up to me. Again, I didn't compete at the level I had earned. I was still paid a little for being on the team—considered a pro athlete—but I didn't compete. The LA Reign didn't extend my contract for the next season, which was for the fall of 2016.

Don't forget: In the fall of 2015, I had started serving as a high school life group leader at Cornerstone. My GRID combine and season experience had encompassed the spring and summer of that year. And in the spring of 2016, Clay had asked me to come on staff at FCA. I had let GRID go and was mentally and emotionally trying to make the shift to starting a life in ministry. I was hard at work that summer trying to raise support funds to be able to make this FCA dream a reality, which wasn't going particularly well.

On a Friday in July 2016, I was heading out of town, traveling to LA to visit some friends for the Fourth of July holiday weekend, when I received a call from the LA Reign. I hadn't spoken with them in several months.

"Josh, we're doing a third season. It's all in Utah. Every team is going to live together, and we'll film all the matches—the whole thing—in Utah over a couple of months. We want you back. We'll pay you twice as much as before and guarantee you a spot on the active roster—$20,000 for the two months."

My heart rate ticked up, and I gripped the phone. A burst of adrenaline punched through my body.

"But you have to sign the contract by Monday," they added.

"Okay, let me get back with you," I said, as the tingling sensation continued to flow from my head to my toes.

Part-way through my road trip to LA, I stopped off in Fresno to see a good friend, Kris Ammons. That Sunday, I went to Kris's church with him, his wife Rachel, and their family. Every waking second between that phone call and that church service, I was weighing the LA Reign's offer. I knew if I accepted it, I'd be rubbing shoulders with elite athletes and hanging out with Buddy Hitchcock and others. Perhaps most tempting, I knew *I'd* be considered an elite athlete too.

The issue . . . I'd have to go to Utah from early September through the month of October. I had just finished the onboarding process to join FCA as a staff member. I had not raised my support yet, and the huddles would kick off in early September, alongside the start of the students' school year. I dwelled on the commitment to FCA and the youth I would minister to as an FCA staff member.

Yet, the competitor in me wanted to prove that I could compete in GRID, and I was battling the painful memories of being benched in the past. I wanted to *show everybody* who and what they had shot down, replaced, ignored, rejected, abandoned, and left behind. Those memories—from the high school summer camp midnight workout to being benched at the start of my senior year at Yale, and from the bogus forty time that left me hanging out to dry with the scouts to being cut from the Texans—they all haunted me. I wanted to prove to every naysayer that I was worthy of being a pro athlete, in any sport in which I set my mind. From missing the CrossFit Games by ten pounds to being benched after making the GRID team, I wanted to rub the world's face in my success.

Guys, I know these are fightin' words. That's how I felt, that I had to fight for myself, my reputation, *my worth*. I wanted redemption for the agony of all those "almosts." Looking back now, I realize that deep down, I just wanted to *belong*.

My flesh, fueled by the need to be redeemed in the world's eyes, thought, *It's just a couple of months. The money is great, and I haven't even raised much money for my FCA support yet. Maybe I can use the GRID money to help me get started with FCA when I get back.* My medical sales success had recently taken a downturn when one of our products was no longer covered by Medicare, so I felt I needed the money the GRID League had offered me.

But, on the flip side, I didn't want to let FCA and the high schoolers down either. The purpose I had found in ministry created a crossroads in my heart.

I was really wrestling with this decision. So I got on my knees and prayed . . .

RED ZONE CHECK

1. What do you make of my need to belong at all costs? To find my identity in sport? Do you see how that need was born from a pattern of rejection, from countless people telling me I wasn't good enough or fast enough? That I didn't have what it takes? That pattern had played out over two decades of my life. The flip side of these messages from the world was pride, selfishness, and idol-worship of me. What other outcomes could have been produced by this type of story? Do you know anyone who struggles with these things? Do you have similar battles? How do you cope? Is it in a healthy or unhealthy way? (Romans 6:6–8)

2. Describe a time when half of you wanted to do something, but you were wrestling in your spirit with the 'right' thing to do? Was God part of this decision in your life? How do you determine the will of God in your life? What did you choose? How did it play out? (Proverbs 16:9)

Chapter 21

THE JOURNEY

Give up the struggle and the fight; relax in the omnipotence of the Lord Jesus; look up into His lovely face and as you behold Him, He will transform you into His likeness. You do the beholding; He does the transforming. There is no short-cut to holiness.

Alan Redpath

As I dressed for church at Kris and his wife Rachel's house, I wrestled and prayed with the decision. Two realms were at war, the physical and the spiritual.

Once we arrived at church, I sat in the congregation, waiting for the speaker. Then, I heard a sound, something like humming. *A motor?* I turned and watched as a man in an electric wheelchair approached the microphone. I noticed he was fully strapped in, including his head, the restraints preventing him from bouncing or being jostled out of the chair by the movement. When he got close to his designated spot at the foot of the stage, someone walked over and moved the microphone so that it sat right in front of his lips. Then, this man started to speak.

He explained he had been diagnosed with ALS (a progressive disease that leaves the body paralyzed but the mind intact) a little more than a year before. Until then, he had been leading a normal life, active and able to do anything. "Now, I'm confined to this wheelchair. I've lost control of everything except my mouth and my lungs. I can breathe, and I can talk," he said. Not a single noise could be heard from those of us rooted to our chairs in the congregation.

"I know now that I want to use every breath I have left to lead people toward Jesus. My last breath, no matter when it comes, will be for Christ. My goal is to have the name of Jesus on my lips when I pass into eternity. Until then, every day, I pray for God to give me as many opportunities as possible to keep doing what I'm doing. To keep breathing and keep talking, to keep pointing people to Him."

As he spoke, tears streamed down my face. God was pricking my heart and soul. In my spirit, I felt His convicting words settle into me:

Josh, the answer is FCA. That's My plan. You are supposed to mentor those young people. You know this. You felt My call. But don't worry, Josh. I'm going to provide. I'll give you everything you need. You know I will do just that if you trust Me. Yet you still want to go play in this GRID League, and you know why, don't you? To prove yourself to the world. Maybe even to make a lot of money. Those are all the worldly reasons to go, yes. You have all of the excuses, don't you? But Josh, I want to know: When are you going to lay all of that down? When are you going to submit to Me? When will what I think of you and My purpose and love for you be enough, Josh?

With each fresh tear, God's message washed over me. Remember, I had been through this convicting season before. I had already released my idol of football; I had been reborn with the identity of Christ before—or so I had thought.

But Satan had tempted me again . . . I was still seeking my identity in athletics, measuring my worth by the measures of worldly success found in CrossFit and the GRID. I was still trying to prove I was good enough. And in that church, sitting next to Kris and Rachel as we listened to this man living well—living with purpose—despite ALS, God's truth spoke again. *There is no eternal significance in what the world defines as treasure. What is the point of all that you are chasing, Josh? That stuff is temporary. It doesn't matter. If you're truly mine, your treasure lies with Me—your eternity with Me.*

> *Do not lay up for yourselves treasures on earth, where moth and rust destroy and where thieves break in and steal, but lay up for yourselves treasures in heaven, where neither moth nor rust destroys and where thieves do not break in and steal. For where your treasure is, there your heart will be also* (Matthew 6:19–21).

Pursuing goals is not bad; athletics and sport are not inherently bad, but it's when they become idols that we fall into disgrace. This is true for any idol. My mom often says, "What you don't find time to do right, you find time to do again." I had fallen before, and yet, there I was again, doing the same thing with CrossFit and GRID that I had done with football. I knew they had become my gods. Not only that . . . my pride and ego were fighting for human acceptance, forgetting I already had God's acceptance. Satan had put the bait right in front of me, and like a hungry fish, I had jumped out of the safety of the *Living Waters* to gobble it up.

Josh, when are you going to give me everything? When will I be enough?

"Now. Now, Lord."

I didn't want to be like the people of Judah to whom Jeremiah the prophet spoke in the Bible, those who continually ignored God at the crossroads. Or turned their backs on Him in defiance. I didn't want to be someone who would not walk on His good paths—who wouldn't believe, love, and obey in all things.

> *Thus says the LORD: "Stand by the roads, and look, and ask for the ancient paths, where the good way is; and walk in it, and find rest for your souls. But they said, 'We will not walk in it'"* (Jeremiah 6:16).

I dropped my head, and my shirt caught fresh tears. I knew at that moment, I was going to turn down the GRID League contract.

The LA Reign establishment was shocked when I said, "No, but thanks," a few days later.

At the end of August, 2016, I started at FCA as a part-time staff member. I hadn't yet raised much money, but I knew God would provide. Even when I didn't have the money to claim the hours I worked, I submitted fewer hours on my timesheet and served, trusting God.

As people watched me serve and saw my commitment, they came alongside me in support. Cornerstone Church became one of my biggest financial supporters. Their youth director, Clint Rutledge, who helped me get started sharing my testimony, as well as my friend and mentor, Matt Warner, went to bat for me. Cornerstone made FCA their primary high school campus ministry outlet for all five of their locations. Then Joe Gibbs Racing came alongside me and supported me. Joe Gibbs, his sons—J.D. and Coy—and current president, Dave Alpern, and team chaplains, Bob Dyer and Hudson Belk, all love Jesus, and they decided this was one way they could give back to the Kingdom. I will be forever grateful.

I continued working for Sam in medical sales, but again, those sales and revenue numbers continued to dwindle. Our topical pain medication was now not reimbursable through any insurance, including for those with diabetic peripheral neuropathy pain, like my dad. That product had made me a lot of money over the years, but doctors stopped prescribing it when insurance dropped it completely.

Sam still had a profitable business with spine implant sales, but his distributorship contracts were for specific regions only—my area of Northern California was not one of them. Sam wanted to keep me, though. I had been his leading salesperson for three years and we were great friends, but keeping me meant asking me to move. I wasn't going to do that. Not after finally understanding my God-given purpose at FCA and having just started there.

In early 2017, I was thriving at FCA and loved witnessing young people come to Christ. I was sold out for FCA's mission because it is a Kingdom mission—one filled with truth, that loves on kids, and that encourages them to be the best versions of themselves. All of this got me up and out of bed in the morning.

But this purpose and my spiritual thriving weren't paying my bills. It just was not enough to support myself. So I prayed about that too.

"God, should I move for Sam and continue to do medical sales? If you want me to do FCA here, I need some help. Please provide a way."

Shortly after initiating that prayer, I attended an FCA huddle at Granada High School, which was my "home high school" for FCA. After turning down the GRID contract and fully committing to the call of mentoring youth, I felt it might be a good time to coach again. I started as a walk-on, part-time consultant, just to help and be around the kids. Tim Silva, the head coach, who deeply loves the Lord, was the one who ran the FCA group for the high school. He's now retired, but man, he was such a great mentor and role model for the kids. He ran a rock solid program that won football games but also focused on building men of character.

Usually, I would book the speakers for the FCA meetings. That week, Coach Silva had said, "I have a guy" and given me the speaker's name. I had never met him, so I wrote the name down. When I got to the huddle early to set up the sound system and food, to blast the worship music and ensure the pizzas arrived in time, this guy tapped me on the shoulder. He introduced himself to me, and the name he used was not the name I was expecting. Confused, I asked, "Who are you?"

"I'm Pastor Darren Anderson from Sunset Community Church. I'm here to share."

"Oh, I thought our speaker was [another name]."

"Yeah, he got sick. So Coach Silva called me to be his replacement, so here I am!"

Here I am, Lord.

I didn't want to be short or brush him off, but I had to keep moving. Kids were arriving, and I wasn't quite ready. "Okay. Cool. I'll introduce you after the opening prayer," I said, as I ran off to check on the pizzas.

With all of the chaos erupting around the room, I still didn't have Pastor Darren Anderson's name in my head. For that reason, when it was time to introduce him, I called him by the first speaker's name—the one who was sick! I was flustered and knew I was not making a great impression. Pastor Darren laughed it off and graciously corrected it when he came up to take the microphone.

Afterward, I was surprised when he asked me out to lunch. Pastor D (what I would later learn everyone calls him) and I had an unexpected conversation. It was as if two kindred spirits were together. He was dynamic, a high-energy guy like me. At the end of our lunch meeting, he said something interesting. "Josh, I don't know where this is going to lead, but I feel it's a divine appointment. At the very least, I know we'll be really good friends."

"Okay, wow. That's awesome. I'd like that."

I left, and in my quiet times with God, I continued to pray about my financial position, that God would pave the way for me to do more than thrive spiritually. It was very much like a Garden of Gethsemane prayer: "God, what is going on? God, don't let me suffer (financially) so that I feel as though I can't do this anymore . . . but no matter what, I trust You." I filled my heart with Scripture:

For you know that the testing of your faith produces steadfastness. And let steadfastness have its full effect, that you may be perfect and complete, lacking in nothing (James 1:3–4).

A week later, Pastor D asked me out to coffee. Apparently, he didn't really drink coffee at all. He thought I liked it, so we met at a Coffee Bean café. Sitting across from me in that tiny shop, with the smell of roasted coffee beans permeating the air, Pastor D offered me the youth pastor position at Sunset Community Church.

I felt overwhelmed, certainly surprised. "That sounds incredible, but I feel called to FCA," I answered him.

"I don't want you to leave FCA. You are doing exactly what I want my youth pastor to do. You're engaging kids at their level. You're building relationships, and I support you doing it. All of it. You'll have a free pass as the youth pastor for any time you need to handle FCA responsibilities. Go do them. And you can do this also."

It seemed too good to be true. I knew there might be other obstacles, so I folded my hands on the table and continued:

"Okay, but number one, I'm not ordained or licensed to be a pastor."

"Oh, we'll take care of that. We'll send you to Global University to get your education, and we'll help you through the process to get licensed."

"You'll pay for my schooling?" I sounded incredulous because I was. "Okay. Great. Thank you. But there's another possible sticking point. Pastor D, I'm divorced. I know some churches don't want pastors who have been through that; it's frowned upon."

"Josh, we serve a God of grace, and who would I be to not offer anyone the same grace that has been given to me?"

I hugged him and thanked him. He told me I still needed to interview with the Board, and I told him I wanted to pray about it.

"One last thing," I said as we moved toward the exit. "I would really love to come see this youth group that I would potentially be leading. Is that possible?" He agreed and invited me to the next youth group meeting. We both left the coffee shop filled with excitement.

At the next youth group meeting at Sunset Community Church, nobody knew who I was—except some stranger playing basketball with the kids before the group officially started. I'm sure they were wondering, "Who is this crazy adult?" as my typical, hyper-competitive self knocked the ball away from a few of the girls to win a game of Knock-Out. Some things never die.

Josh Clark, Pastor Darren's brother-in-law, had been leading the youth group on a part-time basis. He introduced himself, and then I stood off to the side once the meeting started.

Minutes later, I was rocked by the youth worship team. They were off-the-charts amazing, and I don't just mean their talent. I saw the spirit with which they worshiped. In most youth group gatherings, more than half of the kids are standing in the crowd with their hands in their pockets, simply listening to the music. But these kids at Sunset Community Church were sold out. Every one of them had their hands in the air and sang their hearts out. Worship leader, Daniella Reyes, who is now worship leader for the whole church, was unbelievable that night—anointed.

Daniella sang a song by Jesus Culture called "You Won't Relent." The words floated from her lips to my heart, and I was overwhelmed by the Holy Spirit. Just like in my friend Kris's church, as the man with ALS spoke, I heard God talking—not audibly, but in my heart. I felt Him saying, *You're right where I want you.*

Everything that's happened, your whole life, Josh—every success, every failure, the divorce, the highs and lows, the career changes, your brother's death, the people you've met—all of it was leading you to right now.

No longer are you a pride-filled athlete.

No longer are you a pride-filled husband.

No longer are you chasing the wrong things.

You are finally humble enough to be used by Me.

I first gave my life to Jesus when I was five years old. It is a precious memory, one of kneeling with my dad by his bedside. He led me through the Sinner's Prayer. When I prayed for Jesus to be my Lord and savior, I truly meant it. But as you can see, my journey has taken me through ups and downs and highs and lows, and my submission to Christ has wavered. I never stopped believing in Him and never walked away from Him completely, but I have wrestled with God, at times holding on to idols and wanting to do things my way. The Christian life is one of growth, refining through fire and wading ever deeper into the waters of His love and grace.

Sometimes, we know our destinations, our destinies. And sometimes, we don't. We just have to trust the path God lays out. In either case, we each have a journey to undertake. The journey will be grueling. Grit and fortitude will be required, especially when Satan knocks on the door, his hands full of the temptations and lies he aims to use to thwart our progress. But the journey is exactly what we need to mature and become the people—the leaders—God wants us to become to do His Kingdom work. The journey itself, all of it, including the obstacles, pain, and disappointment, is exactly what we need to fulfill our destinies.

> *Blessed is the man who remains steadfast under trial, for when he has stood the test he will receive the crown of life, which God has promised to those who love him* (James 1:12).

I could finally see my entire journey up to that point with 20/20 vision. My destination, my calling, had been laid bare, and I felt the relief and joy of the redemption I had been so desperately seeking. God never relented, even when I had repeatedly messed up. Finally, at that moment, in that worship set, I was standing right where I was supposed to be. *I belonged.*

Worshiping among those teenagers, I wept with a hundred different emotions. Josh Clark noticed me, and he walked over, laid his hand on me, and prayed for me.

For the next year and a half, I felt right where I needed to be. God was transforming me from the inside out and blessing the ministries He entrusted me with.

The Sunset Community Church youth group grew almost immediately. I started with a core group of mostly pastors' kids. These kids really loved the Lord and had already built solid relationships. Their faith journeys had deep roots—and they actually read their Bibles. These youth knew how to worship God, and they were hungry to discover an even more vibrant relationship with Him.

I continued to coach football at Granada High School. One young man, Zack Macintire—whom we called Mac—had become one of the best high school players I ever coached. Mac was that rare combination of great talent, exceptional leadership and character, that is also your hardest worker. He was even voted team captain as a junior. Mac had come to the youth group a year or two before—even attending church when his parents didn't—so when he became a leader of our football team, Mac recruited other football players to attend the church youth group meetings. I watched as God used Mac's and my faith to open doors—to reach more kids.

With FCA, I started with just six high schools. The next thing I knew, I had FCA huddles with eighteen different schools. Every day, I would start at Sunset Church in the mornings, run from one school to the next for lunch huddles; then, in the afternoons, I'd high-tail it to football practice. In the evenings, I'd run back to the youth group at Sunset. It was so much fun.

I experienced countless little wins for God's Kingdom, including a young man, Josh Shapland, who I had led in that first high school life group with Cornerstone back in 2015. He came back on summer break from college to help serve under me in the youth group at Sunset and pour into the next generation. It felt as if God was patting me on the back, saying, "Well done, good and faithful servant" (Matthew 25:21). God ensured my growth personally, professionally, and spiritually. I had been living more of a secular life while doing medical sales and participating in CrossFit, but I found myself up to my neck in intimacy with God. The full-time ministry work challenged me—in all good ways.

Every week, as I prepared the message for the kids, God would confront me, either during the week or immediately following the message, asking me—testing me—to live out the message I was preaching. These were God-inspired challenges whereby God seemed to say: "Okay, Josh. You can talk about this lesson, but can you live it? Is your heart really with Me or are you just telling other people to live righteously? Are you 'walking the talk'?" God took me through these questions, convicting me in different ways. And it was good.

In my first few months at Sunset, Pastor D asked me to preach a sermon to the entire congregation. He wanted the parents of the kids I was leading to know me too. He wanted me to grow. So in early July 2017, I gave the message at Sunset Community Church, and my parents came to hear me preach.

After I finished, Pastor D came on stage and invited those who were struggling to come up, to lay their burdens at the foot of the altar. My dad was one of the first people to come. He fell on his knees, then his face, weeping. I don't even know what was going on with him, but I know he landed at God's feet and was wholly submitted to Him. I saw a repentant heart. It was beautiful.

On a Friday night in February 2018, I volunteered with Tim Tebow's "A Night to Shine," a prom organized for kids with special needs. I was an escort, or date, for one girl attending the prom, and then I stayed after to help clean up—which put me home around 2:00 or 3:00 in the morning.

Saturday mornings were my time to sleep in. That's when I would catch up with some rest, and everyone knew it, particularly my family. They always told others, "Don't call Josh early on Saturday!"

That Saturday morning after the prom, my phone rang at about 8:45 a.m. I rolled over and silenced it, noting the caller ID. My dad. *What is he doing? He knows I was up late!*

Less than a couple of minutes later, it rings again. *DAD.*

I silenced my phone again. I was not feeling it and frustration brewed.

I laid back down and tried to get back to sleep. About fifteen or twenty minutes later, my phone rings again. I sit up and grab it. Now, it's my mom calling. My gut checked itself. *This is abnormal,* I realize. So I answered it.

What I heard was shocking, even hard to describe. My mom was frazzled, seemingly in shock, but crying. She tried to explain what was happening in quick bursts. "Your dad's not breathing. They're doing CPR. He's not coming back. He has a DNR [do not resuscitate order] for anything else . . . I can't do it. I can't do this . . . You talk to the doctor."

What?

In the next instant, a doctor is on the phone. "Josh, your dad is not breathing. We've been working on him for nearly thirty minutes. We've been able to get a heartbeat a few times, but he can't maintain it. Odds are, if we are able to bring him back, he'll have severe brain damage. What do you want me to do?"

I couldn't speak for a few seconds. How does one prepare for a moment like this? I realized this doctor was asking me to let my dad die.

I had no idea what to do. I had just spoken to my dad a couple of days before. He had texted me the day before. He was fine! Now, suddenly, my dad was dying—*may already be dead.*

I choked out some words. "My dad's a fighter. I know that if he could be brought back and live, he'd want that. Give it one more shot; if he doesn't come back, you can call it and let him go."

The doctor hung up. I buried my face in my pillow and wept, crying "the ugly cry" and soaking my pillowcase. I cried out to God to bring my dad back. After several minutes of intense prayer, I sent some messages out to my brothers to pray for Dad.

Fifteen minutes later, I received a message from Mom. It was a message that would forever change our family. *Dad is gone.*

RED ZONE CHECK

1. What do you think the qualifications are to be used by God to do His Kingdom work? (1 Timothy 3:1–13; Titus 1:6–9, note that these are biblical requirements for elders, not just to be a servant of Christ) Do you think God can use you, right now, right where you're at in your journey? Pray that God will equip you with what you need to be bold, lead others to Christ, and share the Good News of the gospel. (Luke 21:14–15, 1 Corinthians 2:13)

2. Do you believe in coincidences? What might really be happening when people talk about coincidences? Come up with your own definition of ***coincidence***. Here's mine to help you brainstorm: *The events we know occur because of God's providential influence, even if the world labels them as luck or fate.* (Romans 8:28–29) Can you think of times in your life where things fell into place and you felt in your spirit that they weren't just by chance? Talk to God about these times; if you see His divine influence, thank Him for His faithfulness.

Chapter 22

THE RACE

Do not be lazy. Run each day's race with all your might so that, at the end, you will receive the victory wreath from God.
Basilea Schlink

You can never truly prepare yourself for someone to leave your life—this life—especially someone who is so pivotal to it. Death is the weirdest thing.

Over the last year, I've had the privilege of speaking at four memorial services. I say *privilege*, because it's a heavy burden but a poignant joy. Funerals and memorial services are places no one wants to go, let alone speak, but I believe it's a responsibility to honor the people who have passed. In my case, we've honored my brother, my dad, my aunt, my niece, my cousin, and my great-uncle, thus far. Yes, it's a privilege. You want to take the responsibility seriously, but you also want to celebrate the lives of your loved ones, honor them, and give thanks for every moment you had with them. And you want to point people toward the hope we have in Christ. Those are my goals when I speak.

When I arrived back in Florida on an early morning flight from California, my oldest brother, Jerry, picked me up from the airport. When I walked into the house, my mom collapsed into my arms. Together, we mourned the loss of my dad. It was all just so shocking.

Then my mom tells me the story:

After I had instructed the doctor to try one more time to resuscitate him, my mom took Dad's hand as they worked on him. As she held Dad's hand, the physician called his time of death, and the healthcare professionals shut everything down. Mom told Dad how much she loved him. How he had done everything he could to pour into his family and lead us toward Jesus throughout his entire life. And that we were going to be okay. At that moment, my mom felt like he was there, in the room, and could see her—not his mortal body but his spirit, looking at her. I don't know the reality of that; I haven't experienced something like that. But she told me that she said to him, "Jerry, you can go. Go be with Jesus." Mom said that as she said those words, a tear slipped down Dad's cheek, and then he was gone.

There's so much to say about my dad. I was lucky, surely blessed, to be called his son, to have that position in life. I realize people have all sorts of relationships with their parents, but as much as my dad drove me crazy and at times, some of the things he did frustrated me, I can say that without a doubt, that man loved me. And loved me hard. He was there for everything. Any time. Any place—including my senior year in high school when he took those four months off from work to attend every football game and practice I had.

Dad always wanted to talk about Jesus. During my college years, when I'd get home late at night, he'd be sitting up, studying his Bible in the middle of the night. He called it his "Night Watch," and he wanted to tell me all about everything God was showing him.

"I'm tired, Dad."

"Okay, Son."

When I woke up the next morning and trudged downstairs, Dad would already be up. He had already gotten his coffee, and was primed to talk about those deep, theological things he had learned in the silence of the night. And if I was the first one up, I became his audience—it was a bit overwhelming. I wasn't even ready to speak yet, but he was there, modeling for me his passion for Jesus, loving me and the rest of our family, and showing everyone how God and family were his priorities (in that order).

He was a fiery man in the best of ways. Dad had a temper, and I've battled that proclivity (sin) too, but he cared deeply about the things that mattered. He invested himself and touched a lot of people. Dad had a habit of making people feel seen. He knew how to empathize and connect with people. He was "fearlessly affectionate," as our dear family friend, Jerry Regier, said in his message at my dad's funeral. Dad was not a shallow man, but a man who built intimate relationships.

The most treasured part of Dad, though, was his burden to share the gospel and his love of Jesus, to proclaim the truth of who God is and what that means for His plans for our lives. He had a heart for and of worship. That is what this book is for me—an act of worship. A way to share my God-story and glorify Him. My dad had always wanted to write a book, to outline his God story too. I have thousands, if not hundreds of thousands, of pages of his journals. He never got around to it, but maybe someday, I'll write his book using those journal entries.

At his memorial, I spoke about how Dad ran his race well. How he could finally rest, knowing he lived his life in such a way that he could say:

> *I have fought the good fight, I have finished the race, I have kept the faith* (2 Timothy 4:7).

After his passing, I opened my dad's phone and saw the last Scripture he had meditated upon on this earth: Hebrews 6:19, which says, "We have this hope as an anchor for the soul, firm and secure . . ." (NIV). He had talked to me about that hope many times before. Even when his faith was tested with the passing of my brother, even when he wondered if that tragedy would cause him to turn his back on God and wake up the following day with a different perspective about God's love and goodness, my dad told me, "The anchor held, son. The anchor held."

I pray your anchors hold too.

My dad ran his race well. When his life ended, it became the next generation's time. *My time.* Not my time like it's my time to do what I want. No. It became my time to submit my life completely to Jesus and let Him use me to the fullest measure and for every intention He has for me. To bring forth every spiritual gift. To release all of the baggage I carried.

To let go of this focus, which I had held onto for so long:

I'm going to shape myself into someone who can't be turned down or cut. I'm going to be the best, so no one can say no. I'm going to transform my body to avoid rejection and abandonment and show those who told me I wasn't good enough that they were wrong. I'm going to be charming and make myself into something women want. I'm going to approach the prettiest girl and get her to choose me.

That's the flesh talking, influenced by Satan, no doubt. Those were the thoughts I had; that was the life I had been living. It's what I did. All of those statements weren't my thoughts all at once. They occurred over many years, but God had to break me of all of that to be able to use me the way He wanted—in ministry. And that breaking is actually a sweet mercy by God, to kick out from under us all the worldly things we use to prop ourselves up, that will *never* really satisfy, until all that's left is Him.

But make no mistake. My flesh is still alive and active. In Romans, it says when we accept Christ, we put our old personas aside; we die in some sense. That's true. But, later in the book of Romans, it says we still live in these mortal bodies and so while we've been delivered, we will keep being tempted, we'll keep having to fight the tendency to fall backward into old patterns of thought and action. We need help. We can't overcome sin with pure willpower. We must love Jesus more than our sin.

To the best of our abilities, we're all called to run our races well, to do what my dad did and submit ourselves to God, our heavenly Father, so He can do more than we ever think or imagine is possible.

RED ZONE CHECK

1. What's the biggest loss or disappointment you've faced in your life? How did this event change you? Can you see God at work even in the midst of hardship and pain? (Psalm 34:18)

2. What are the biggest victories you've ever achieved or the most joy you've ever felt? Did you get there on your own? Or were these blessings that God gave you out of His kindness and mercy? (1 Corinthians 15:57, Deuteronomy 20:4)

3. How would others describe the race you are running right now? Are you stumbling? In last place? Giving it your all? What are you running toward? What's your goal or purpose? What do you want people to say about you when your race is done? (1 Corinthians 9:24–27)

Chapter 23
THE DESTINATION

The best use of life is love. The best expression of love is time.
The best time to love is now.
Rick Warren

It's my time.

The title came to me about three-quarters of the way through writing this book. God impressed upon me the idea of my dad passing the baton, relinquishing his race, and it now becoming *my* race. My dad had a saying: "Don't be too heavenly-minded for any earthly good," meaning don't be so caught up in the nuances of theology or so committed to private, intimate time with God that you aren't actually loving and serving the people around you. My dad was passionate about his beliefs, but he deeply loved people and was a relational individual. This legacy requires big shoes, but with God, I aim to fulfill the goal and finish my race well too.

God is the author of our stories. He's the one who bends us, molding us into the children He has destined us to become, should we accept the call. God has special plans for each of our races, and His plans should trump our own—always.

This is my story, but it's not about me. It's about God and what He has done in my life. The purpose of these chapters is not to show how great I am, but to outline how God used me for His glory. Even when Satan meant harm, even when evil seemed to prevail, even when my own flesh and sin interrupted the journey, God was there, growing me and using those hardships for His purposes. God's plan will be forever victorious. And that should provide comfort and hope.

> *For those whom he foreknew he also predestined to be conformed to the image of his Son, in order that he might be the firstborn among many brothers* (Romans 8:29).

It's *my time* to share how God conformed me (and continues to do so) to the image of His son, Jesus. I've learned that our biggest trials become our ministries. No tear is ever wasted. No circumstance can't be used for good.

I've had the unparalleled privilege of talking to many men who were on the verge of divorce. And I say privilege because it's a blessing to be used by God—that He has placed me in a position to pour into their lives at a critical moment. I've never counseled them to leave or said, "It's over, just move on." My discussions with them are filled with the notion and encouragement that they should fight for their wives. I remind these men, just as I had to learn, that they can't change their spouses. That's never the goal or the point. The challenge I offer is the one my mentors gave me: Submit to Christ and repent. Put your focus on Christ and make the focal point of your life about serving Him and bringing Him glory through loving others well—especially your spouse. It's the only way our God-given hearts can love the way He designed, being enabled to do so by the power of the Holy Spirit in and through us. I also challenge them with the call of marriage, especially for the men, to lead their spouses toward Christ by loving sacrificially. To honor the Lord God first and foremost as the great designer of marriage, to hold to the covenant they made on their wedding day. Though God may allow for divorce because of the harness of our sinful hearts, that is not His good and perfect provision for us. We are not supposed to separate what He has so beautifully woven together. So, stop looking for a way out and start looking at your own heart. Believe me, I know the soul-crushing fallout of not doing it God's way. I pray others can learn from the mistakes I've made and the lessons God has taught me through them.

After years of singleness post-divorce, God granted me the overwhelming blessing of a bride once more. Traci Ruth Carroll and I were married on May 28, 2022, on a picturesque day just before sunset on a private beach cabana in Siesta Key, Florida. Traci is far more than I could have ever dreamed or imagined. She loves with an intensity and passion that I have never known. Her generosity and gentle affection overflow from the Holy Spirit inside of her. Most amazingly, she grants me grace, underserved grace, time and time again when I fail to emulate Christ's sacrificial love. I see Jesus in her, and I'm convicted of my own sin—not through accusation, but through love. In this way, her love refines me and helps me continue to grow into the man God made me to be.

God is so good. He is a God of restoration, and He will heal what is broken inside of us if we trust Him enough to fully give it all to Him. My dad wrote me a letter shortly before his death, one that was lost and forgotten. A couple of weeks after he passed, I found it and was overcome with emotion as I read it. I wept as I took in his bittersweet, beautiful cursive words, inscripted in dark ink from a classic fountain pen on the special parchment paper. The letter contained so many messages that any son would long to hear from his father: words of praise and encouragement, apologies for mistakes made, predictions for my future serving Christ, and, of course, love. One line stood out. He said, "Jesus Christ will restore what the locusts have eaten." He is referencing a Bible verse, Joel 2:25, where God promised to mend the broken nation of Judah, giving back what had been taken as a result of their sin and rebellion. My dad was saying that God would restore in my life what my sin and selfishness had taken, specifically a wife and a family. This was the prayer that my father had been lifting up but also a statement made in confident faith. Traci never got to meet my father on this earth, but his prayers were answered. I believe Jesus wants to restore in all of us that which our sinful locusts have eaten away.

My primary ministry is all about discipling youth. I love coaching kids because of the unique role that it affords me in their lives. Whether I'm working with them on general athleticism, strength training, speed and skill development, or conditioning for football, I'm giving them tools to grow. But I'm also building relationships, and though I care about how well they do, based on their own goals, I care way more about their hearts and where they will spend eternity. Sports are such a great metaphor for life. The obstacles to overcome, hard work that pays off, the pressure-packed learning experiences, and coming together as a team for a common goal greater than self-interest are all valuable lessons. God is our ultimate coach and Jesus, our trustworthy teammate. My mission is for people to see God's plan for their lives. To help them discover how God is refining and preparing them for their future ministries—just like He did for me through sports and other athletic endeavors.

My focus, my destination if you will, is Jesus. This Son of Man was mocked, stripped, beaten, and crucified. He knows pain. He felt betrayal because he was betrayed multiple times and by those closest to him. He endured suffering, torture even. And he died for us. Yet, despite all of that, some of his last words to our Father, while he hung on that cross, asked Him to forgive us. For none of us knows what we're doing in this world.

You see, we're all just hurting ourselves, thwarting our own progress. We see a destination we think is perfect. We set our sights on something of this world, be it a goal to play in the NFL or win a Pulitzer prize or earn a billion dollars. Even if it seems like a noble goal—like raising a family or opening a business, it's not—unless it's from Him. Once the goals are set, we habitually choose our own paths, rejecting God's way at every turn. We think we know better. And in doing so, we pave the way to our own destruction.

Thankfully, there is hope, even when we have chosen poorly. We can overcome Satan and all that he intends. How? By the blood of the lamb and the word of our testimony.

> *And they have conquered him by the blood of the Lamb and by the word of their testimony, for they loved not their lives even unto death* (Revelation 12:11).

This book is the testimony of what God has done in my life. Others may have more rags to riches stories or powerful testimonies of overcoming what seem to be more difficult struggles. I thought I was better than my brother Jacob because I didn't struggle with the same things he did—addiction. Maybe I looked better on the outside (or thought I did), but what God has shown me is that I have the same heart problem we all do. We all rebel in different ways, but ultimately, we're all aiming for control. We all have the same God story. We all choose ourselves over God at some time or another (or often). We all think our way is better than God's way. It's the tried-and-true sin of selfishness, born in a garden, and that involves a piece of forbidden fruit. We all carry the sin of self in our hearts, wicked as our hearts are (Jeremiah 17:9). Maybe my symptoms differ from yours, but we all need heart transformations. Every day.

If we will actually read God's Word, everything we *need* is there. We have enough information. We can see His purposes are good. We know in our hearts that His plans are perfect. But we wrestle with God over the details of how our lives should play out. The solution is humble repentance and complete trust in Him. We may have to repent hundreds of thousands of times along the way, moment by moment even, as He mercifully kicks out the props and crutches we use to bolster our circumstances or our egos.

As we submit, we can *endure* all things through Christ, who strengthens us (Philippians 4:13). This Scripture often gets misquoted and misused. Though the translated Greek word *ischyo*, in its simplest form, means *do*, in this context, it conveys the concept of *enduring*. Paul wrote this right after mentioning being content in all circumstances—whether well fed or hungry, whether living in abundance or in need. It's not that we can do all things in terms of accomplishing whatever we wish or desire. The point that Paul is making is he is able because Christ enables Him. Anything that he accomplishes, any work done for the Kingdom, is only done because of the grace and mercy of Christ.

Jesus is the one that enables us. More importantly, regardless of achievement, if the venture looks like worldly success or provides personal comfort, we that are in Christ can not only soldier on but rejoice. I know athletes (and others) use this verse all the time—to justify chasing after a Super Bowl win, for example. I was this athlete. I wanted to lead my team to victory, to claim glory, and then give God all the praise when a reporter put a microphone in my face. Jesus Christ should get *all* of the praise and glory, for the Lamb is worthy, and we certainly can't accomplish anything without Him. But we can't just rubber stamp our every desire with this (or any other Bible verse). Our desires are not holy just because we want them.

Paul is imploring us to choose joy and to actively worship and give praise, regardless of our circumstances. That is what Christ has been teaching me all these years. I have repeatedly risen and fallen with my circumstances. But now, it's *my time* to fully submit to *His time*. It's time to grab that baton and ready it for the next generation—you.

Again, we have all the knowledge; now, it's time to act. Maybe it's your time to accept Jesus as your Lord and Savior. Perhaps it's your time to share your testimony. I don't know. But I do know this: It's *everyone's time* to follow God in all ways and through all things.

So let this moment, this season, this life be *His time* for you.

RED ZONE CHECK

1. Do you have enough knowledge so that it's now time to act? If not, where can you gain the knowledge you need of God to drop everything else and jump into His plan for your life? If more knowledge of Him is not the answer, then what is the block in your heart that is preventing you from making Him the Lord of your life? If you know God well and have the understanding of His infinite love for you, what is holding you back from being all-in for Him? What can you do today to surrender your way for His? (Deuteronomy 10:14, Galatians 2:20)

2. Write down the lies you are believing about yourself, about God's love for you, and about how others may/may not see you. Then, take those lies and turn them around to write the truth of the who God says you are. (Romans 8:15–16, 2 Corinthians 10:3–5, Romans 12:2)

Chapter 24

THE CONCLUSION

I hunger and thirst for God's Word. He comforts my soul in my sorrow and stirs up my joy with His promises. God's Word reveals Jesus to me, and as I walk in His presence, I find strength and courage for my journey. God knows my heart, and I seek with all that is within me to know God's heart as well.
Jerry D. Phillips (Dad), inscribed in his Bible on May 18, 2007

This passage wraps around me as the warm embrace of both my dad's love and my heavenly Father's incomprehensible grace. It is such a sweet reminder of Dad's love for Jesus. But it also grounds me because I know how flawed my dad was—as am I. This was my dad's heart . . . to be repentant, wholly submitted, strike a blow for Christ, even with His last breath.

However, I know all too well how often he failed at that in his flesh. Yet he kept bringing it back to the foot of the cross, bringing his failures and sins, as well as his hopes and dreams, to lay at Christ's feet. This is why King David was called "a man after God's own heart" because he was truly repentant. I aspire to run my race as well as Jerry D. Phillips and to be a man completely surrendered to Jesus Christ—a man after God's own heart. To say that I miss my dad is a massive understatement. I think about him every day, and there will forever be a Dad-shaped hole inside my heart. But his legacy lives on in me, in the way that I move forward and make the time I have left here count.

I have taken the baton, and I will run my race with fervor and passion, for *it is my time*. God has revealed that my time is really *His time*. The only way to run this race to win is to run it for Him and His glory alone.

> *For physical training is of some value, but godliness (spiritual training) is of value in everything and in every way, since it holds promise for the present life and for the life to come* (1 Timothy 4:8).

My prayer for all of you who are reading this book is that you are convicted by the Holy Spirit, convicted of the ways in which you are still doing it your way. In addition to Satan's manipulative schemes, we are masters of lying to ourselves. One of my dad's most fervent prayers, late in life, was for God to help him stop lying to himself, to show him where he had been deceived. I continue to pray that very prayer for myself and for all of you.

We can't run the race wholeheartedly for Christ until we see the places that we have yet to completely submit to Him.

This process is ongoing, similar to my football journey. At every level that I moved up to, from high school to college and finally pro, the speed of the game increased, and I learned what it would really take to compete at that level. Every step that we take with Christ will reveal how much deeper our trust and faith in Him needs to be and where we are lacking. This is sanctification in a nutshell.

God continues to refine me. *Hallelujah!* He hasn't stopped working on me yet.

My competitive fire still burns bright. I continue to compete in Masters Olympic Weightlifting, taking second at US Nationals in 2021 and qualifying for World Championships in 2022. I am also the head football coach for Sarasota High School and assistant coach for the boys' weightlifting team. I love competition. I have from the time of my earliest memory. I don't think competing is inherently wrong, and I want to encourage all of you to continue to set goals and chase after them with zeal. But I challenge you to ask yourself: Whose glory are you really doing it for?

> *Do nothing out of selfish ambition or vain conceit, but in humility consider others better than yourselves. Each of you should look not only to your own interests, but also to the interests of others* (Philippians 2:3–4).

Trust me, I have to ask myself this question repeatedly. As each new season of life comes, and my goals change and shift, the Holy Spirit is grinding off the rough edges of my heart and guiding me to make every plan His plan. You may think, well then why do you keep setting athletic goals? Aren't these all fleeting, worthless, like chasing after the wind?

I would say no, they aren't of *no* value, but their value is not in whatever weight or significance society attributes to them. Their value is in how they can be used for the Kingdom to impact others and bring Christ glory. God can garner glory out of anything, even the smallest act. Everything we do can be an act of worship, even the most menial task, like cleaning a bathroom. Everything matters! So then, the question becomes: *Is this goal more important to me than God?*

The goal itself might not be bad, or sinful, but if we love the gift more than we love the Giver, it is an idol for us. Remember, Galatians 6:4 says, "Pay careful attention to your own work, for then you will get the satisfaction of a job well done, and you won't need to compare yourself to anyone else."

I think a great test for our heart's position on any issue is the tightness of our grip on it. Are we holding it with an open hand? Are we willing to let it go? What is our identity without it? We see this in the Old Testament when Abraham is asked to sacrifice the thing that he had waited for, desired for so many years and loved so dearly, his one and only son, Isaac. God tested Abraham's faith by seeing if he was willing to put to death the thing he loved the most. When Abraham relented, it revealed his heart; God knew Abraham's heart and knew what he would do. This test wasn't for God, it was for Abraham. When God stopped Abraham from completing the act and replaced Isaac with a ram, God showed His goodness and faithfulness, and this increased Abraham's faith.

God takes us all through moments like this. I've gone through them over and over again. Staying at Lake Highland my senior year after getting benched, trusting God with my NFL dream after injury and rejection—this book is full of examples. But so too is *your* life. I pray that you ask God to reveal to you all the ways He has been faithful to you. All the ways, over all the years, that He has come through again and again. I pray that as you do that, you are refreshed and encouraged to take another step in faith. To take the places in your life and the moments in time where you think "this is my time" and make them all about Him.

Though I love to compete, the ultimate competition now becomes being better than the man I was yesterday. That doesn't always mean lifting more weight, running a faster time, or having more earthly success. More and more, this measure is an internal one. It's how you react to a given situation or trial. Did I learn from the last time God allowed me to encounter this? Am I growing; am I trusting Him evermore? This is what a *W* really is. Winning is abiding in Him to such an extent that your actions are dictated by complete submission to Him and His will.

> *Do you not know that in a race all the runners run, but only one gets the prize? Run in such a way as to get the prize* (1 Corinthians 9:24).

So run your race well. It is your time . . .

FINAL PRAYER

My final prayer for you is that the following verse can be said of your life, for all your days to come: "For I am already being poured out like a drink offering, and the time for my departure is near. I have fought the good fight, I have finished the race, I have kept the faith" (2 Timothy 4:6–7).

A CALL TO ACTION

This has been *My Time.* Now, it's *Your Time*. Using your answers to the Red Zone questions at the end of each chapter, craft *your* God story—your personal testimony to God's faithfulness as He pursues *all* of you. You don't have to write a full book, but I encourage you to write something. Start a blog, write a devotion, or simply write a journal entry (or several). Then, share your testimony, speaking truth about what God has done in your life, with others. We are mandated by God to share the gospel with the world and the truth of the testimony God has written through our lives with others. It is through sharing these truths that hearts are led to faith in Jesus and the lies of the enemy are overcome. No one else has your testimony; it is unique to you and your life. Your story matters! You have no idea how God will use you or who He will impact through your life. So be bold. Start with some trusted friends or family members; then branch out, as the Spirit leads, and share your testimony with those who either don't know God yet or who are working through their own tough journeys. If you consider yourself a seeker, perhaps curious but not sold out for Christ, I pray my story and these questions have revealed God working in your life and awakened your interest in pursuing Jesus, to find out what knowing Him could mean for you. I promise, it's worth it.

THE RESCUE

I believe in the power of the Holy Spirit to take the words that have been written in these pages and change hearts. By His grace, your eternal future does not depend on me or any talent that I may or may not have to recount my testimony or reveal the truth of the gospel. But your future in eternity requires a response. I would be remiss, with all of the discussion of the gospel in this book, if I didn't actually present it in such a way that you can receive the precious gift of salvation. Since I have been blessed to serve Jesus through FCA, I think it makes sense to utilize the simple but wonderful tool they borrowed from Manuel Leiser, with Campus Crusade for Christ, called The Four to communicate the gospel.

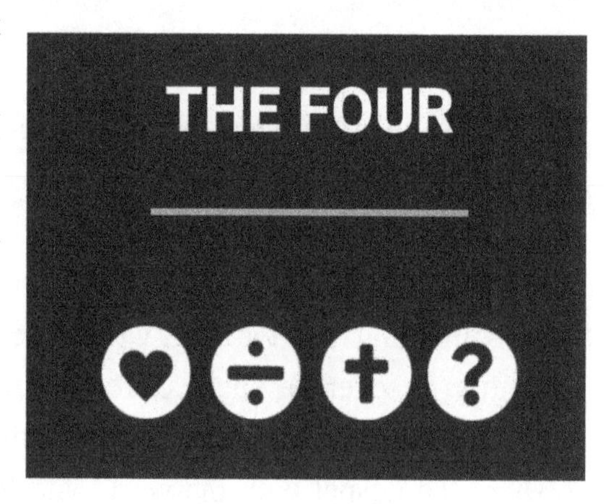

1. **God Loves You**
   God loves you more than you can ever fully imagine or comprehend. He knit you together in your mother's womb, gave you life, has a great plan for your life, and desperately wants a relationship with you.

2. **Sin Separates You**

Our sinful rebellion against God—doing things our way rather than His or thinking we know better—drives a wedge between us and God. He is holy and righteous and cannot be in fellowship with sin. Our sin deserves a just punishment, which is our death—not just physically, but spiritually. However, God loves us so much that He wants to reconcile us to Himself.

3. **Jesus Rescues You**

God Himself, Jesus Christ, came to earth, born of a virgin, to offer Himself as the perfect sacrifice that we could never be. Jesus drank the full cup of the righteous wrath of God as He hung on the cross and gave up His Spirit unto death so that we may be made alive in Him. He rose again on the third day, not only proving He was God, but also defeating death and Satan and breaking us free from the chains of sin.

4. **Will You Trust Jesus**

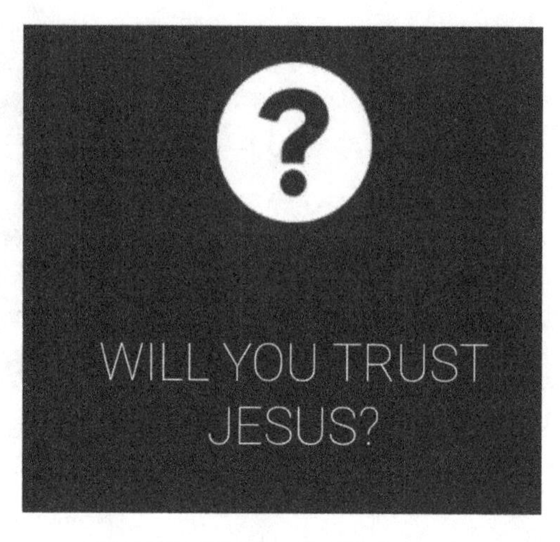

To receive this amazing, incomprehensible sacrificial gift that Jesus offers us, we must respond. John the Baptist came before Jesus as a precursor to prepare the way. He baptized for repentance of sin. It is imperative to grasp the gravity of what Jesus did on the cross, that we recognize that we should be up there instead. That is the penalty we truly deserve. Yet, He loved you enough to endure it for you. We must repent of our sin and turn from it. That pivot is from self-reliance to total trust and faith in Jesus Christ.

"If you declare with your mouth, 'Jesus is Lord,' and believe in your heart that God raised him from the dead, you will be saved. For it is with your heart that you believe and are justified, and it is with your mouth that you profess your faith and are saved" (Romans 10:9–10).

That declaration is not just an acknowledgement that we know who Jesus is. The demons and Satan all know who He is, but they refuse to submit to Him and will not make Him their Lord. Confessing "Jesus is Lord" is an outward expression of a submitted heart position where you put Jesus Christ back on the throne of your life, where He belongs.

If you want to receive the gift of salvation and make Jesus the Lord of your life, I encourage you to pray this simple prayer:

"Jesus, I believe you are the son of God, took on flesh, lived a sinless life and took the punishment that I rightly deserve. That you rose from the grave on the third day, conquered sin and death, and will come again. I want to repent of my sin and turn from it. I need you. I need you to change me from the inside out. You are the Lord of my life. I love you. Help me serve you and bring you glory all of my days."

These are not magic words. The prayer of salvation can be prayed a lot of different ways and that's really not the point. God knows your heart and if you've actually chosen to give your life to Him or not. If you just prayed this prayer, Hallelujah! This is the best and most important decision you will ever make in your life. Angels in heaven are literally celebrating right now and singing in praise because when you depart this life, you will live in eternal fellowship with God.

But it doesn't end here. You are going to need help to walk this walk. We were never meant to do it alone. That is why God created the Church. I encourage you to find a Bible teaching, Christ following church near you and get plugged in. You need to be discipled by other, more mature believers. You also need to read the word of God for yourself. If you truly love Him, you will want to know Him and you will desire to follow His ways. Getting connected to the Body of Christ, reading His word, and talking to Him daily in prayer are essential parts of life in Christ. God bless you on your journey. I'm praying for you.

GET CONNECTED

If you want to go deeper in your faith or find tools to help you take those initial steps down the path that will lead you closer to Christ, I encourage you connect with me (or my team at Faith Forge). Go to faithforge.org and find discipleship materials, instructional videos, blogs, podcasts, and more. Faith Forge is a forum, a platform where Christian men and women provide content for other believers to sharpen their faith. Our goal is to help you forge inner strength and courageous character through the refining fire of the Holy Spirit and to equip you through Jesus Christ for spiritual battle. We are in a fight, and the enemy has come to steal, kill, and destroy. Arm yourself for battle and don't wage the war alone.

Feel free to reach out to me directly with a prayer request or even a theological question at josh@faithforge.org. Stay plugged in through whatever social media outlet best suits your needs:

Website: faithforge.org
Instagram: @faith.forge
Twitter: @faithforgeorg
TikTok: @faithforgeorg
Facebook: Faith Forge
YouTube Channel: Faith Forge

PHOTO GALLERY

Mud Bowl MVP and Little League Champion
at 11 years old.

The Baby of a weird but wonderful family.

Senior year at Lake Highland Prep,
shaving my head was a BAD choice.

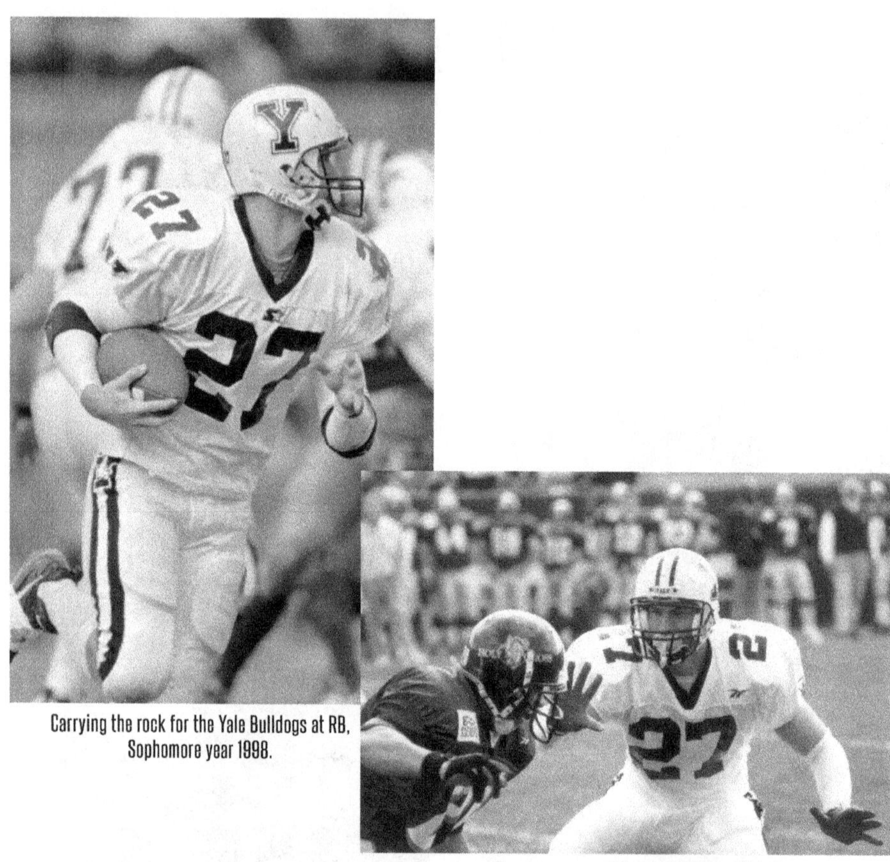

Carrying the rock for the Yale Bulldogs at RB, Sophomore year 1998.

Press coverage at Corner for Yale vs Holy Cross.

Dad (Jerry), Mom (Judy), me and my brother (Conard) at University of San Diego.

Always the baby of the family but no longer the "little" brother.
(Left to Right: Jerry, Jay, Conard, Jacob, Me).

Training at my old high school LHP, no pads, no problem, 2001.

A Joyful Introduction for the Amsterdam Admirals 2002

Finally in an NFL Uniform, Texans vs
NY Giants in the Hall of Fame Game 2002.

On the set of "We Are Marshall" with actor Arlen Escarpeta,
who played QB Reggie Oliver.

My 30th birthday with a crew of amazing friends including Chris Ackerman (far left), Brandon Yarckin (second of the left), Josh Holt (behind me), Chandler (arm on my Dad's shoulder) and Josh Reeves (far right).

With my brother from another mother IG, Ivery Gaskins.

Hitting the Big Snatch at NorCal Crossfit Regional Competition in 2014 with my CSA Teammates.

The Eye of the Tiger with my ultimate Crossfit Teammate and training partner Buddy Hitchcock.

Running down my competition rep by rep doing thrusters in Grid League tryouts 2015.

On the rings where I won my spot of the Grid League, Los Angeles Reign.

Last family shot taken, Thanksgiving 2014. (Left to Right: Jerry, Me, Mom, Dad, Sheryl, Jay, Conard).

Finally finding my calling, leading young people to Christ. Praying on the National Day of Prayer with two of my youth, Nathaniel Anderson and Dani Reyes.

Coaching is a ministry as well. Making in game adjustments as the Defensive Coordinator for the Manatee High Hurricanes in 2022.

Jesus blessed me with an amazingly loving Christian wife, Traci Ruth Phillips, May 28th 2022.

ACKNOWLEDGMENTS

Completing *It's My Time* and getting it published is the culmination of a lifelong dream. I realize none of this was done alone. God has surrounded me with *people* whose love, support, and encouragement have been pivotal in enabling me to become the man I am today. *It's My Time* is a testimony of God's faithful hand in writing my life's story.

My family is a wonderful, messy blend of personalities, steeped in godly values, with West Virginia Mountaineer hillbilly roots. I thank my tireless, servant-hearted, meek mother, Judy Phillips. Her love is boundless and embodies the mercy of Jesus Christ. No one has more consistently believed in me and encouraged me to chase my dreams. Without you, Mom, none of this would have been possible.

To my two older brothers, Jerry and Jay Halstead, for their belief in what God has been doing in and through me. Thank you for your faith in God and trust in me to be a good steward.

Joe Gibbs Racing has faithfully supported me as an organization since the beginning. Joe Gibbs and his sons, JD and Coy, spearheaded efforts to support numerous charities and godly ministries, including for FCA and me. Tragically, both JD and Coy have gone home to be with Jesus Christ, well before what we would have thought was their time.

We will see them again in heaven, as their faith was strong and their fruit was evident in their lives.

JGR's president, Dave Alpern, was generous enough to write the Foreword for *It's My Time.* JGR has two in-house spiritual leaders and chaplains, Bob Dyer and Hudson Belk, who have shown unwavering support for me and my ministry. Thank you, all.

I got my start in ministry while serving at Cornerstone Fellowship (CF) Church in Livermore, CA. There, Matt Warner counseled me and walked me through how to pick up the pieces of my life. Then Clint Rutledge asked me to share my testimony with the youth group and subsequently encouraged me to start sharing my story at local high school FCA clubs. Thank you both so much for your faith in me and helping FCA East Bay make a huge impact.

Thank you to FCA Leader Clay Elliott and his wife, Kelly, for pouring into me and helping me get my feet on the ground. Former Regional Vice President Mark Boyer, Barry Martinez, Otis Amey, Rigo Lopez, John Goulding, Whitney Elliott, Matthew Decker, Josh Jackson, and my first FCA hire, Jared Furze . . . thank you for serving alongside me, for being soldiers for Christ and ambassadors of the gospel.

To all the youth pastors in the East Bay who gave your time to support local high school FCA huddles and equipped your youth to lead, thank you: Brandon Westphal, Steve Sanderson, Samuel Laws, Trevor Van Kempen, Jake Rexroad, Scott Bodenhamer, Josh Clark, Joey Manzi, and so many more.

Brian Atchinson, though facing terminal cancer, expressed a burning desire to serve Jesus and spread the gospel with every breath he had left. Thank you for touching my heart and striking one more blow for Christ, Brian.

Pastor Darin Anderson believed in me enough to support me taking the giant leap into full-time ministry and enabled me to become a pastor. And to my entire Sunset Community Church family for being a true church family in every imaginable way. Thank you, and I love you all.

One couple, Don and Sally Meredith, were instrumental in helping me see God's calling on me. They have been faithful supporters not just in FCA but throughout many of the toughest and most challenging moments of my life. Don also passed recently, and Sally still counsels my wife, Traci, and me. I can't say enough about how much they mean to my family, but I believe they know how we feel.

Jerry and Sharyn Regier are also foundational members of my home team. They were founding members of Potomic Chapel in Virginia. We love you all dearly and you will forever be family.

Several of my dad's close personal friends jumped in to support my efforts to raise support. Manning Herr, Eric Kempthorn, Steve and Jeanine Hammond . . . thank you all for your faithful giving and for honoring my father's memory through me.

Bill and Carolyn Salter have become like parents to me. I'm close friends with their boys, Blake and Todd, but they treat me like blood. Thank you all for your consistent, sacrificial support, loving spirit, and spiritual warfare on my behalf.

Thank you Coach Tim Borcky and Reverend Joe Sims for making a critical impact on my life at a crucial time. To Coaches Jack Sielecki, Rick Flanders, and Larry Ciotti, thank you all for putting an encouraging arm around me when I needed it.

To my agents, Kyle Rote Jr. and Matt Schultz, for taking a chance on me. Thank you to Charlie Casserly for giving me the chance to prove myself in NFL Europe and signing me.

To my NFL Europe coaches, thank you for believing in "crazy white" and for providing one the best experiences of my life. Bart Andrus, Jeff Reinebold, and Larry Owens, I will forever be grateful for the journey.

Dom Capers and Joe Marciano, thank you for letting me down gently and for your class. Joe, thank you for the uplifting words on the way out; those will stick with me forever.

To Mike Hohensee, thank you for seeing the warrior in me and for elevating me off practice squad.

To all my Lake Highland Prep teammates, the high school experience shaped the man I am today. Brian Hoffman and Mike Verille, thank you for pushing me to be better and giving something to shoot for. Scott Appleman, thank you for being a consistent loyal friend and for letting me borrow your helmet. Quentin Freeman, thanks for making me your QB1 and for watching all those Orlando Magic games with me while eating my mom's cinnamon toast.

My best friend from LHP and lifelong brother is Brandon Yarckin. Thank you for making me part of your family and always being there, no matter what.

To my Yale teammates, thank you for showing me how to build something from the ground up. We turned a 1–9 rookie campaign into a 9–1 Ivy League Championship. Pat Graham, Billy Artemenko, Jake Fuller, Chris Larson, Michael McClellan, Justin Jacobs, Ray Littleton, Paul Ardire, Timothy Whitsett, TJ Hyland, Ben Johnston, and so many more . . . thank you all for being faithful brothers in Christ. John Hardie, thank you for leading our Athletes in Action group on campus and encouraging me to go to AIA Camp. That time made a huge impact on me. To my Yale brothers that have passed, you are missed, and your spirits live on in us: Peter Mazza, Ryan LoProto, Jim Kepple, and Terrance Hobson.

To my NFL Europe teammates: Mike Sutton, Blaine McClemurray, and Kevin Daft thank you for your friendship, encouragement and the nickname.

To my Texan teammates: David Carr, Matt Stevens, and Aaron Glenn, thank you for showing me what a professional football player looks like.

To my Chicago Rush teammates, thank you for teaching me how to play a different game and walking with me through the loss of my brother, especially you, Sam Clemons. Thanks for your laser focus in life and for always being there when needed.

Growth takes challenge and there were men who challenged me along my journey to step up my game. Quadry Ismail, Desmond Howard, and Chris Carter, thank you for inspiring me and taking the time to mentor me. And Ivery Gaskins, you are a brother for life and in eternity. Thank you for your iron strength, faith, and leadership.

Thank you, Coach Walter Hameline for believing in me and for giving me so much responsibility as a young coach. Effrain Martinez, thank you for trusting me to coordinate your defense and guiding us to a Conference Championship. Dr. Marcus Elliott, thank you for seeing more than an ex jock who would train people, for guiding me to be a sport scientist. Mike Blasquez, thank you so much for bringing me to the PAC-12 and let me help you build something.

Coach Jeff Tedford, thank you for making and supporting me as a Cal Bear. Kevin Knox, Chris Disanto, Ron Gould, Ron Coccimiglio, Andrew McGraw, and Matt Weigand, thank you for being brothers in Christ in a secular world and a competitive environment.

To Coach Tim Silva, Coach Greg Wiliford, and Coach Jacquez Green, thank you for letting me learn and lead.

To my Manatee brothers, Brian McCloy, Doug Schofield, Dennis Stallard, Tripp Allen, Kavious Price, Terrace Dunbar, Willie Brown, Steve Ross, Josh Weirich, Snoop Carter, Jason Heidel, Tziah Conley, Dominique Dunbar, Tracy Sanders, Bon Bean, Jim Nelson, especially Bowen Summer, Chad Choate and Mayor Gene Brown, plus all of the support staff and volunteers that make Manatee Hurricane football go, thank you.

To my new Sarasota High family thank you for believing in me. Thank you Principal David Jones and the head coach search committee for giving me my first Head Coaching job. Thor Miller, Russell Hann and the rest of the previous staff thank you for believing we have what it takes to build a championship program.

There is a special place in my heart for all the players I've coached over the years at every level. Zack Macintire and Josiah Knight at the high school level. Giorgio Tavvechio and Bryan Anger at Cal.

Thank you, Florida FCA Board: Brooke Corbett, Frank Brunner, John Booth, Kami Pentecost, Jeff and Meme Signor, Dean Weirs, Jerry Marlar, Evelyn Mangann, Pastor Luke Stockland, and Matt Ennis.

Thank you to my beta readers: Landon Pentecost, John Wingate, Sally Meredith, Zack Macintire, Alex Brunner, Jaden Hamilton, and Dani Reyes.

My endorsers, thank you for taking the time to read it and for putting your name and reputation behind it: Dave Alpern, Clint Hurdle, Anthony Randall, Dominic Herbst, Andrea Ager, Sally Meredith, Jerry Regier, Zakk Uhler, Michael McClellan, Chris Rix and Giorgio Tavvechio.

This book would not be possible without my amazing publishing team at Morgan James. Thank you for believing in me and for giving me an opportunity to share the story of what God has done in my life. Special thanks to Cortney Donelson for all your contributions to this process. Your skill and guidance took this dream and made it a reality.

Last, but certainly not least, are my group of close friends who have carried me through this life, making me a better man. You bless me, Brandon Yarckin, Chris Ackerman, Blake Salter, Ivery Gaskins, Zakk Uhler, Sam Clemons, Josh Reeves, Josh Holt, Kris Ammons, Travis Ortega, Brian McCloy, Buddy Hitchcock, Nick Zambruno, and Chris Connolly. Love you all!

To my wife, Traci Ruth, you are the answer to my prayers, a help mate beyond compare. Your tender heart, boundless service and affection bless my life.

ABOUT THE AUTHOR

Josh Phillips is a Christ-following, fiercely competitive coach and pastor. He is driven to inspire others to be the men and women God created them to be through finding their identities in Christ and putting their complete trust in Him. Josh is a former NFL football player, multiple-time CrossFit Regional competitor, drafted GRID League Athlete, and USA Weightlifting competitor. He graduated from Yale, where he majored in Psychology, minored in Religious Philosophy, ran track, and played football. He holds two masters' degrees: a Master's in Business Administration from Wagner College and a Master's in Kinesiology Biomechanics from Cal State, Northridge. Josh's research, "Effect of Ankle Joint Contact Angle and Ground Contact Time on Depth Jump Performance," was published in the *Journal of Strength and Conditioning Research*. He has coached at the University of California Berkeley, University of California Santa Barbara, Wagner College, Los Angeles

Pierce College, the Peak Performance Project (P3), and multiple high schools. He is currently the head football coach at Sarasota High School and assistant coaches weightlifting while teaching in the Physical Education Department. He is also the founder of Faith Forge, a ministry dedicated to leading others to forge inner strength and courageous character through the refining fire of the Holy Spirit, while equipping them in Jesus Christ for spiritual battle. Josh is a speaker and relishes the opportunity to share the testimony of what God has done in his life. He calls sunny Sarasota, Florida, home, where he enjoys working out, bowling, beach escapes, and golden lattes with his beautiful, godly wife, Traci, and their cats.

A free ebook edition is available with the purchase of this book.

To claim your free ebook edition:

1. Visit MorganJamesBOGO.com
2. Sign your name CLEARLY in the space
3. Complete the form and submit a photo of the entire copyright page
4. You or your friend can download the ebook to your preferred device

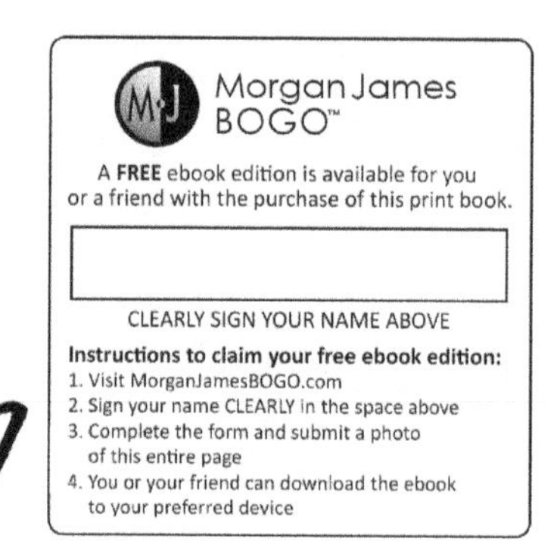

Print & Digital Together Forever.

Snap a photo

Free ebook

Read anywhere

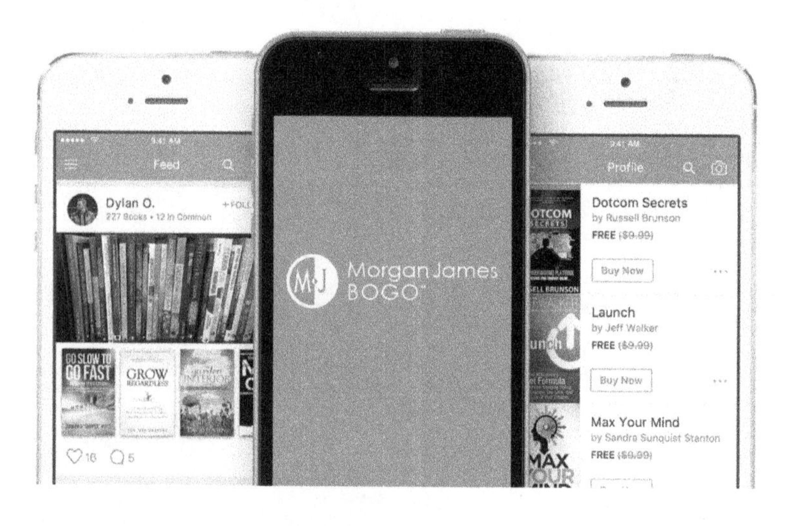